THE IMITATION OF CHRIST

THOMAS À KEMPIS

A Timeless Classic for
Contemporary Readers
William C. Creasy

Christian Classics™
from Ave Maria Press, Inc.   Notre Dame, IN

William Creasy's version of *The Imitation of Christ* is more than a new translation of a timeless work. It's a re-creation of a 560-year-old classic that infuses it with life and meaning for contemporary readers.

Working from the 1441 autograph manuscript, Creasy succeeds in creating a dramatically different interpretation of *The Imitation* by working through its historical, cultural, and linguistic contexts. For Creasy, Thomas à Kempis offers profound insights into a person's relationship with God, insights that only deepen when they accommodate a post-Vatican II understanding of what he has to say.

He accomplishes this by using a technique called reader-response theory, bringing forward the fifteenth-century reader's response to such themes in the work as contempt for the world, the spirit versus the flesh, friendship, and sin, to effectively harmonize them with a twentieth-century understanding.

Yet Creasy's is a faithful translation, even to the point of replicating theoretical devices, stylistic patterns, and figures of speech used by Thomas à Kempis. It provides the reader the opportunity to discover the book praised by Johnson, Carlyle, and Eliot, and translated by Ignatius Loyola; the most widely published book after the Bible; a book that has appeared in over 600 editions and guided millions on their journey to God; a book that offers new insight and deeper understanding with each reading.

William Creasy holds a doctorate in English from UCLA where he is a member of the faculty. His research and teaching interests include manuscript reconstruction and textual analysis, fifteenth to seventeenth century devotional literature, the English Bible, and Renaissance poetry and prose.

First printing, October 1989
Tenth printing, December 2008
82,000 copies in print

www.avemariapress.com

Founded in 1865, Ave Maria Press is a ministry of the Indiana Province of Holy Cross.

ISBN-10 0-87061-231-X   ISBN-13 978-0-87061-231-2

Cover and text design by Thomas W. Ringenberg.

Printed and bound in the United States of America.

Contents

Book 2

Suggestions Drawing One toward the Inner Life

Book 3

Of Inner Comfort

Book 4

The Book on the Sacrament

Preface

During a lifetime of reading we encounter only a few books we keep coming back to, only a few books that offer a new insight or a deeper understanding with each reading. The *Imitation of Christ* has been such a book for me, as it has been for countless others.

I first read the *Imitation* as an undergraduate. I still have the copy, an old Everyman's Library edition edited by Ernest Rhys, a blue hardback that I paid a couple of dollars for in a second-hand bookstore in Phoenix, Arizona. At the time, I wasn't the least bit interested in Christianity, except as background for my academic studies; I had no idea that the book would unleash the Hound of Heaven. But books do that sort of thing: George MacDonald's *Phantastes* did it for C.S. Lewis; Etienne Gilson's *The Spirit of Medieval Philosophy* did it for Thomas Merton.

The *Imitation* captured my attention again during my doctoral studies. An English major, I was especially interested in 15th-century literature and the development of English prose style. And there sat the *Imitation*. It had appeared in English as early as 1470; it was printed in 1503 in the William Atkinson/Lady Margaret Beaufort translation, going through four editions by 1528; and it was translated by Richard Whitford in 1530, appearing in at least 10 editions through 1585. As a vehicle for studying the development of English prose style the *Imitation* served perfectly.

The book entered my life once more during an especially difficult period. Like Dante, "when I had journeyed half of our life's way, I found myself in a dark wood, for I had lost the path." The *Imitation* became a lantern to my feet. I suppose it was inevitable that I one day translate it.

So I have. In my translation I try to mirror accurately the text that Thomas à Kempis wrote; this is the first task of any translator. But I am also very cautious not to produce a stylistically quaint text or one that is far removed from a modern reader's theological or spiritual experience. To my mind, Thomas à Kempis offers profound insights into a person's relationship with God, and those insights only deepen if they accommodate a post-Vatican II understanding of what he has to say.

For the Latin text I went directly to Thomas à Kempis' 1441 autograph manuscript. It is owned by the Bibliotheque Royale in Brussels and is catalogued as MS 5855-61; they kindly supplied me with a microfilm copy. I transcribed the manuscript on to computer disk, checking it against L.M.J. Delaisse's diplomatic edition and M.J. Pohl's critical edition. I also compared the Latin text to the British Library's Royal MS 7.B.VIII. This is one of 18 extant English manuscripts of the Latin text. It is similar to the text that both Atkinson and Whitford would have used. Although I have compared the autograph text to it, I have translated solely from the autograph itself. Variant readings have deepened my understanding of the text, but they have not affected my transcription of it.

I completed most of the translation at the Huntington Library in San Marino, California. It has been my good fortune to be a Huntington Reader off and on for a dozen years; it was my particular good fortune to spend six months in residence during the Fall and Winter of 1986-87. The rich collections, idyllic gardens, and pleasant lunch-hour conversations have taken me as close to paradise as I have come in this world. I would like to thank the Huntington, and especially the staff in Readers' Services, for their kindness, their courtesy and their extraordinary knowledge of one of the world's great research libraries.

With each reading of the *Imitation* I find the book means ever more to me. In part, this is due to the changing experience I bring to the text, and that experience is due for the most part to the people who share my life. For his warm friendship and kindness I would like to thank Br. Luke Armour, O.C.S.O., of Gethsemani Abbey in Kentucky. Brother Luke spent countless hours and gave scrupulous attention to reading the manuscript for this book; his comments have been both insightful and invaluable. Brother Luke is not only a friend, but a well-loved member of my family and a part of our daily thoughts and prayers. I would also like to thank the community of monks at Our Lady of Mepkin Abbey in South Carolina. From my first visit to Mepkin, I felt a part of the community, a welcomed guest and a brother in Christ. Their continued warmth, kindness and hospitality have given me a true spiritual home. I would especially like to thank Fr. Christian Carr, O.C.S.O., Abbot of Our Lady of Mepkin, and Fr. Richard McGuire, O.C.S.O., Br. Edward Shivell, O.C.S.O., and Br. John Corrigan, O.C.S.O., all of whom generously offered their thoughts on the *Imitation*. I would like to thank, too, my dear friend Lisa Smith, whose own following of Christ has taken her from the corporate board room to the church, from designing financial products to caring for the homeless and the poor. Lisa is a model of courage and commitment, one who has heard Christ's words and has acted on them. And as usual, many thanks must go to John X. Evans, Michael Cohen, OM Brack, Robert S. Nordlie, and Fr. Robert Rivers, C.S.P. With their own talents, each has helped me understand the *Imitation of Christ* a little better, but I thank them most especially for their steadfast friendship. It was John Evans who said that a friend is someone who has known you for 20 years and loves you anyhow; it was Michael who agreed and the others who applauded.

Finally, I wish to thank my wife, Lynette, and my sons, Adam and Jonathan. With me from the start, they have been patient beyond reason, supportive beyond hope, and loving beyond measure. St. Francis de Sales tells us that love is the abridgement of all theology, indeed, is grace itself. In Lynette, Adam and Jonathan I have been graced beyond all deserving. I dedicate this book to them.

William C. Creasy
Westwood
Easter, 1989

Introduction

For several years now the *Imitation of Christ* has been an important book to me. As a student of medieval and renaissance literature, I have studied it as a major work of 15th-century devotional literature; as a late 20th-century Christian, it has played an important role in my own spiritual development. Yet, surprisingly, when I mention the *Imitation* to my academic colleagues, more often than not they have never heard of it; when I mention it to my clerical friends, they usually think back to their seminary days when they read it and then dismiss it out-of-hand as a hopelessly pre-Vatican II book, full of contempt for the world and self-loathing. If Vatican II opened the windows of the church to let in some fresh air, the breeze seems to have blown the *Imitation* into a corner and covered it with dust; if anyone pays attention to it these days, it is the attention paid to a museum piece.

For a book accorded nearly universal praise for over 500 years, it is a curious state of affairs. Consider its history. Written in the Netherlands between 1420 and 1427, it made its way through Europe in Latin, French, German, Italian and Spanish in more than 100 printed editions by the end of the 15th century. In England, it saw 46 editions in six translations before 1640. During the 18th century Samuel Johnson remarked to Boswell that it "must be a good book, as the world has opened its arms to receive it. It is said to have been printed in one language or other, as many times as there have been months since it first came out."[1]

In England the *Imitation* seldom went without praise. St. Thomas More recommended it as one of three books that every Christian should read. Samuel Johnson confessed to a group of visitors toward the end of his life that "I feared that I had neglected God, and that then I had not a mind to give him: on which I set about to read Thomas à Kempis in Low Dutch, which I accomplished, and thence I judged that my mind was not impaired."[2] Thomas Carlyle sent a copy to his mother on February 13, 1833, with a note saying that "no Book, I believe, except the Bible, has been so universally read and loved by Christians of all tongues and sects: it gives me pleasure to fancy that the Christian heart of my good Mother may also derive nourishment and strengthening from what has already nourished and strengthened so many."[3] In a letter to Sara Sophia Hennell on February 9, 1849, George Eliot says that she has "at last the most delightful *de imitatione Christi* with quaint woodcuts. One breathes a cool air as of cloisters in the book—it makes one long to be a saint for a few months [!]. Verily, its piety has its foundations in the depth of the divine-human soul."[4] Her appreciation shows, too, in *Mill on the Floss* (Book 4, Chapter 3), where the *Imitation* comforts Maggie Tulliver:

> She read on and on in the old book, devouring eagerly the dialogues with the invisible Teacher, the pattern of sorrow, the source of all strength; returning to it after she had been called away, and reading till the sun went down behind the willows.... The old-fashioned book, for which you need only pay six pence at a book-stall, works miracles to this day, turning bitter waters into sweetness.... It is the chronicle of a solitary, hidden anguish, struggle, trust and triumph.... It remains to all time a lasting record of human needs and human consolation: the voice of a brother who, ages ago, felt and suffered and renounced...under the same silent far-off heavens, and with the same passionate desires, the same strivings, the same weariness.[5]

Thomas De Quincy praises the *Imitation*'s "slender rivulets of truth silently stealing away into light,"[6] and Matthew Arnold calls it "the most exquisite document, after those of the New Testament, of all the documents the Christian spirit has ever inspired."[7] Only William Thackeray, as far as I know, shows a crotchety ill will toward the *Imitation*. In a letter to Mrs. William Brookfield on Christmas day, 1849, he says:

Why, you dear creature—what a history that is in the Thos.
à Kempis book. The scheme of that book carried out would
make the world the most wretched useless dreary doting
place of sojourn...a set of selfish beings crawling about
avoiding one another, and howling a perpetual miserere....
We know that deductions like this have been drawn from
the teachings of J.C.: but Please God the world is preparing to throw them over.[8]

In spite of the *Imitation*'s history and the esteem in which it was held
by most people for half a millenium, many people today echo Thackeray's sentiments. And I suppose that is understandable. A classic
though it may be, the *Imitation* was written by a man in a cloister for
other cloistered men, and it was written in a time and culture far removed from our own. When a person with even the best of intentions
picks up a copy of the *Imitation* and reads that "this is the highest and
most profitable lesson: truly to know and to despise ourselves" or "this
is the highest wisdom: through contempt of the world to aspire to the
kingdom of heaven" he or she is likely to put the book down again, perhaps calling to mind the documents of Vatican II, especially *Gaudium et
Spes*, where we are all urged to a "growing awareness of the sublime
dignity of the human person" and the responsibility of the Christian and
the church in a world that "has been created and sustained by the love of
its maker, which has been freed from the slavery of sin by Christ...so
that it might be fashioned anew according to God's design and brought
to its fulfillment.'"[9] In light of Vatican II, most readers today are likely
to wonder how people could have clung to such depressing and mistaken
notions for so long a time.

If we are to appreciate the *Imitation* today, perhaps we need to take
it out of the corner, dust it off, and read it anew. For a start, we need to
confront its historical, literary and theological problems head on. We
shall find plenty of them. Historically, the problem of authorship looms
largest, so let us start with that. The *Imitation* has seen its share of false
ascriptions. Whole books have been written on the topic, each aggres-
sively backing its own candidate. Deep into the *Imitation*'s "authorial
problem," a reader is frequently tempted to invoke the author of the
Imitation himself, whoever he may be: "Do not let the writer's author-

ity or learning influence you, be it little or great, but let the love of pure truth attract you to read. Do not ask, 'Who said this?' but pay attention to what is said.''[10]

Historically, the *Imitation* has been linked to St. Bernard of Clairvaux; St. Bonaventure; Henry Suso; Ludolph of Saxony, the Carthusian; Ubertino of Casale; Pope Innocent III, with whose *De contemptu mundi* the *Imitation* was confused; Johannes de Canobaco; Walter Hilton, author of the *Scale of Perfection*, one of the books that St. Thomas More recommends; Jean Gerson, Chancellor of the University of Paris; Giovanni Gerson, a man thought to have been Abbot of the Benedictine monastery of Santo Stefano in Vercelli, northern Italy; Gerard Groote, founder of the Brothers of the Common Life; and, of course, Thomas à Kempis.

Thomas à Kempis, who lived to the extraordinary age of 92 (c.1379-1471), was a prolific copyist and writer. Born in Kampen, Thomas followed his brother John to Deventer in order to attend the city school. There he encountered the Brothers of the Common Life, followers of Gerard Groote's New Devotion. Thomas attended school in Deventer between 1392 and 1399. He then traveled to Zwolle to visit his brother, who was by that time Prior of the Mount St. Agnes monastery. He probably entered the monastery on that visit, although he was not invested until 1406. He was ordained priest in 1413/14. Thomas never left the Mount St. Agnes monastery, except for the years 1429-1431, when the community chose to live in exile rather than to disobey a papal interdict imposed on the diocese of Utrecht, and shortly after, when he traveled to Mariaborn near Arnhem to care for his brother, then Superior of the House of Bethany, who had become seriously ill and who died on November 4, 1432.

His long life proved fruitful. He copied two bibles, each in 10 volumes,[11] and several missals and choir books. He also wrote many treatises, hymns and historical works, including the lives of Gerard Groote, Florens Radewijns, John van de Gronde and John Brinckerinck, all of whom were active in the ''New Devotion''; a chronicle of the Mount St. Agnes monastery; and a life of St. Lidwina of Schiedam. His most important works, however, were a series of sermons to the monastery's novices and several devotional treatises, including *Prayers and Medita-*

tions on the Life of Christ, Meditations on the Incarnation of Christ, Of True Compunction of Heart, Soliloquy of the Soul, Garden of Roses, and *Valley of Lilies.* Crowning the list are the four *Imitation* treatises, bound with nine other works in Thomas' 1441 autograph manuscript, now in the Bibliotheque Royale in Brussels, catalogued as MS 5855-61.[12] It is rather hard to find. English translations are also available for individual works, but they are scarce also. Thomas never claimed authorship for any of his works, including the *Imitation*; the autograph manuscript ends in a colophon simply stating: *Finitus et completus anno domini m.cccc.xli. per manus fratris thome kempis in monte sancte agnetis prope zwollis.*

It is the *per manus fratris thome kempis*—by the hand of brother Thomas of Kampen—that causes all the problems: Did Thomas write the *Imitation* or did he simply copy it? In spite of all the ink spilled over the problem, we shall probably never know for certain. Personally, I find the work of scholars on Thomas' authorship quite convincing. In addition, I have transcribed and edited the Latin text of the autograph manuscript and translated the *Imitation* into English from that edition, and I have also studied Thomas' other works with great care. I see his fingerprints all over the autograph pages. In both style and content the *Imitation* fits with Thomas' other works; one can cross-reference themes and even exact phrases and sentences from one work to another; and one can find an abundance of similarities in syntax and prose style between the *Imitation* and the other works that Thomas clearly did write. But even with all this, suggesting a high degree of probability is the best we can do: Thomas à Kempis *probably* wrote the *Imitation of Christ*; until stronger evidence to the contrary comes along, I shall follow tradition, placing his name on the title page.

Whether Thomas wrote or only copied the *Imitation*, it was published in the typical medieval fashion: One person passed it to another, copied it, then passed it on again. The earliest dated manuscript of Book 1 appears in 1424 and another appears in 1425. All four books appear by 1427. Scholars have shown that the text was continually developed and edited until the Thomas à Kempis 1441 autograph manuscript, at which point it stabilized. The manuscripts that found their way into England, and thence into English translation, usually contained only Books 1-3, some contained only Book 1, and only a few contained Book 4. Eighteen such Latin manuscripts current in England during the 16th century still exist.

The *Imitation* was first translated into English during the second half of the 15th century, probably by an anonymous Carthusian monk of the Sheen Charterhouse. Four manuscripts of that translation survive. No English translation was printed for the general public until 1503. At that time Lady Margaret Beaufort, Countess of Richmond and Derby and Henry VIII's grandmother, commissioned William Atkinson, Doctor of Divinity and prebendary of Southwell, to translate the *Imitation* from Latin into English. Atkinson translated Books 1-3; Lady Margaret herself translated Book 4 from a 1494 French edition. When St. Thomas More recommended the *Imitation*, he was probably thinking of the Atkinson/Beaufort translation; it had been available for nearly 30 years in four editions.

In addition to its being the first printed English translation of the *Imitation*, the Atkinson/Beaufort is interesting on another count. In English, its prose style is remarkable; it stands as a wonderful example of the "golden style" so popular at the beginning of the 16th century. Not everyone agreed that such a prose style was appropriate, however, especially for devotional books such as the *Imitation*. Richard Whitford, a close friend of St. Thomas More, criticized the Atkinson/Beaufort version for its ornate prose style and resolved to translate the *Imitation* himself, finding a decorous style that was not "overmoch eloquent, nor in any wise barbarous," and he resolved to translate solely from Latin. He published his translation in 1530, and he did such a good job that it influenced translations of the *Imitation* for the next 400 years. One of the most popular editions of the *Imitation* today, the Image Book edition by Harold C. Gardiner, S.J., is a modern version of Whitford's translation. Father Gardiner even now calls Whitford's work "the perfect rendering of a thing of perfection."

So why translate the *Imitation* again? Since Whitford's translation, nearly 500 editions have appeared in English in dozens of translations. As I write, there are 18 editions in print, ranging from the very literal translation of the Daughters of St. Paul to the poetic but idiosyncratic rendering of Robert Dudly; one can find paraphrases for a modern audience and even an edition in verse. Why have there been so many translations, and why offer another? More importantly, with all the translations and editions to choose from, why has the *Imitation* so clearly fallen out of favor among modern readers; why has it become a book often bought but seldom read?

The answers to these questions, I think, lie not so much in the *Imitation* as in the modern reader. At the beginning of our discussion I gave several quotes to support my assertion that the *Imitation* has nearly always held an honored place among readers of English. Look at them again: Thomas Carlyle fancies "that the Christian heart of my good Mother may...derive nourishment and strengthening" from it; George Eliot "breathes a cool air as of cloisters in the book," and her character, Maggie Tulliver, feels that it "works miracles to this day, turning bitter waters into sweetness"; Thomas De Quincey praises its "slender rivulets of truth silently stealing away into light"; and Matthew Arnold reads pages, across which "skims an ethereal light." None of these comments says a thing about the *Imitation*, but they all say volumes about how a reader *responds* to the *Imitation*. It is a crucial distinction.

Recent critics have written much about how a reader responds to a work of literature. Professor Stanley Fish was one of the first, and he remains one of the best.[13] Fish distinguishes between the text as a physical object and the text as the reader experiences it while reading. For Professor Fish, a text is not a container into which one reaches for meaning; it is an event that one experiences. One does not root out meaning from a string of words printed on a page; one creates meaning by interacting with the words in a sensitive and informed manner. To Fish's way of thinking, a text is meaningless without the reader, just as a dance is meaningless without the dancer. For one who first encounters it, such an idea may seem more than a bit off plumb. After all, a text is a physical thing, ink on a page put there by an author who presumably had a clear idea of what he wanted to say. Besides, it is easy to view the text as an object: my copy of the *Imitation* sits on the bookshelf in my study; your copy sits on your lap in front of you. But is the text a fixed object? While a book sits in my study or on your lap, it is. But when we open it up and read it, *something happens.*

Consider what happens when a "typical" 20th-century reader

meets a particularly troublesome sentence from Book 1, Chapter 1 of
the *Imitation*: "This is the highest wisdom: through contempt of the
world to aspire to the kingdom of heaven." On the surface, the response
follows standard linguistic and rhetorical analysis; beneath the surface,
and at the same time, the reader builds a whole network of associative,
cognitive responses that include, by definition, both awareness and
judgment. This is the highest wisdom. "Ah, ha," thinks our reader,
"I'm about to be told what the highest wisdom is: A (wisdom) = B
(something)." Next he reads, *through contempt*. "Umm," he thinks,
"by means of contempt I'm going to discover the wisdom that sits at the
apex of all wisdom. Sounds pretty doubtful to me; contempt is a mark of
pride. Contempt of what?" *Of the world*, says the text. "Oh, the old
contemptus mundi theme," responds our friend. "Old hat, outdated
stuff. I remember that from a literature course in school. Thank goodness for Vatican II. [Comic motif here: the bumbling, serpentine troop
of monks flagellating themselves in a Woody Allen film, followed
quickly by a twinge of guilt. Sr. Mary Agnes in the third grade said that
monks—holy monks—did that!] *To aspire*. "To have aspirations,"
thinks our reader, "aspirations are good things, on the whole: *through
contempt of the world to aspire to...* What?" *The kingdom of heaven*.
"Good, I'd like to gain the kingdom of heaven, but through holding the
world in contempt? That seems a bit misguided. God so loved the world
that he gave his only begotten Son.... So how did the church ever come
to that contempt of the world stuff, anyhow? If God loved it, what right
have I to hold it in contempt?"

You get the picture. Professor Fish tells us that an "informed
reader" brings to the text a network of linguistic, semantic, literary,
and for our purposes, theological and spiritual experience that allows
him to avoid a superficial or idiosyncratic response to what he reads;
indeed, it is a reader's obligation to become "the informed reader." But
the *typical* reader is not the *informed* reader, as Professor Fish defines
him. The typical reader of the *Imitation* responds like our reader in the
paragraph above; his or her frame of reference is limited by the experience of one who lives in an intensely secular society and who is probably
not a professional literary critic or theologian. Through reading and
study a reader's experience may stretch back through several centuries,

but his or her primary experience rests firmly in day-to-day life. When such a reader encounters *contempt of the world, fear of God, self-hatred, wicked flesh*, and so on, he or she experiences the text in a very different way from an informed 15th-century reader steeped in a lifetime of *lectio divina*, a reader to whom the terms mean something very different.

All this carries profound implications for a translator. When a modern reader complains that the *Imitation* is hopelessly outdated, he is not responding to the text, but to his *experience* of the text, usually as he has experienced it in a translation. Rarely, though, does a translation take into account the reader's frame of reference and attempt to present a text that, given that frame of reference, will produce a response similar to that of the original audience. And this, it seems to me, should be a translator's goal: to recreate for the reader an original "informed" reader's experience of the text. Creating such an experience involves translating not only the linguistic, syntactic, grammatical and rhetorical structure of a text, but also fitting the text into the reader's frame of reference. It becomes the translator's job, then, not so much to translate the text as to *re-create* it. I have tried to do this in my translation. I render our sample sentence, for example, in its full context, as:

> What good does it do, then, to debate about the Trinity, if by a lack of humility you are displeasing to the Trinity? In truth, lofty words do not make a person holy and just, but a virtuous life makes one dear to God. I would much rather feel profound sorrow for my sins than be able to define the theological term for it. If you knew the whole Bible by heart and the sayings of all the philosophers, what good would it all be without God's love and grace? Vanity of vanities and all is vanity, except to love God and to serve only him. This is the highest wisdom: to see the world as it truly is, fallen and fleeting; to love the world not for its own sake, but for God's; and to direct all your effort toward achieving the kingdom of heaven.

Where I can, I echo both the deep structure and the surface structure, even to the point of replicating sentence structures and rhetorical devices, but I do not do so if I think that it distorts a reader's experience of the text, either theologically or stylistically. The final sentence, for example, retains the Latin's surface structure in its first half, but its second half shifts from four prepositional phrases balanced on an infinitive to a series of three phrases which more accurately reflects the "informed reader's" response to *contempus mundi*.

To this point we have spent some time talking about prose style, translation methods, and a reader's response to the *Imitation*, and I think it has been time well spent. The *Imitation*, in its various translations and editions, has touched the hearts and souls of countless men and women for centuries precisely because of the way they experience the words as they are arranged on the page, and lately the *Imitation* has been ignored for the same reason. To my mind, though, a contemporary reader can experience the *Imitation* as deeply and as profoundly as a reader from any earlier time. Our world may change radically in its outward appearances, but as men and women we change little in the depths of our hearts. And it is here that the *Imitation* speaks to us as we walk the world and search for God among our neighbors and in our own inner silence and solitude.

When Thomas wrote the *Imitation*, he saw a world in deep conflict, a world whose foundations seemed to be cracking and crumbling. The death of Pope Gregory XI on March 27, 1378 set the stage for the Great Schism, that rending of Western Christendom that shattered the church for two generations. A week after Gregory's death the conclave met to elect a new pope, and Bartolomeo Prignano, Archbishop of Bari, found himself named Urban VI, against a background of riots and mob violence. He quickly proved himself to be a savage, cruel, repulsive and vengeful autocrat; he probably murdered five of the cardinals who had opposed him. The others fled Rome and reconvened at Fondi, in the province of Naples. There they held a new election and named Cardinal Robert of Geneva to the papacy, crowning him Pope Clement VII on October 31, 1378. Most of the Curia and its staff escaped from Rome and joined Clement. Both men promptly excommunicated each other, and both oiled the machinery of war. When Urban's mercenaries emerged victorious near Marino on April 29, 1379, and when he acquired Castel Sant'Angelo, Clement withdrew from Italy and settled at Avignon, where the papacy had had lavish quarters since 1309. As the struggle intensified, each man forged his political alliances: Urban boasted Italy, the Emperor Charles IV, Hungary, Scandinavia and England; Clement claimed France, Burgundy, Savoy, Naples and Scotland; Germany divided its loyalties between the two. It was the start of a scandal that sapped the moral and spiritual strength of Christendom like an open, infected wound for nearly 40 years. It finally began to heal at the Council of Constance with the resignation of Gregory XII, the deposition of Benedict XIII and John XXIII, and the election by a two-thirds majority vote of Cardinal Oddone Colonna on November 11, 1417, as Pope Martin V.

The ecclesiastical drama of Thomas' world played on a dark stage. The Black Death that had swept Europe like a prairie fire in 1348, killing a third of its population in less than three years, recurred nearly every decade for a hundred years with devastating effects. Each pass of the Black Death—whether it cut a wide, deep swath or only made a narrow, high sweep—sent shock waves to the roots of countless towns and villages. The Netherlands proved no exception. Not a country, but a loose collection of fiefs, some belonging to France, some to the Holy Roman Empire, they were a land of industrial and commercial towns, importing raw material and exporting their products, primarily cloth and copperwork. As in any industrial economy, radical shifts in supply and demand caused equally radical swings in local economies. When the plague swept through Europe, production fell and prices rose; in the Netherlands weavers and fullers went unpaid and butchers and bakers went out of business. Constant wars on the continent compounded the problem, endangering trade routes and forcing import and export restrictions. The wind grew heavy with the smell of class struggle and revolution. The nobles, merchants, and craftsmen—all those with something to lose—savagely repressed local uprisings; then the wind blew in the other direction: The wage-earners imposed a reign of terror in 1379, first in Ghent, then in Bruges, and then in Ypres and all Flanders. To the east, Brabant saw its revolt crushed. Still further east, Liege witnessed a furious revolt earlier on in 1312, during which the wage-earners herded many of the region's prominent folk into a local church and burnt it to the ground with them in it. The Liege revolt raged on until 1384, when the craft-guilds took over the city government and then proceeded to quarrel over it among themselves.

Such was the world that Thomas knew when he left his home in Kampen at the age of 13 and made the long day's walk to Deventer to attend school; it was also the world he walked out of in 1399 when he joined his brother John, who was then Prior of the recently founded monastery of Mount St. Agnes, located about midway between Kampen and Deventer. The monastery provided a haven of tranquility and peace for Thomas, far from the noise and chaos of the world. As I mentioned earlier, he lived 92 years, 72 of them in the monastery, and he only ventured outside the walls twice. Contrasting the world with the monastery, Thomas could say, with Seneca: "As often as I went out among men, I returned less of a man."[14]

When he entered the monastery of Mount St. Agnes, he entered a community shaped by the *Devotio Moderna*, or the "New Devotion," a movement of men and women begun by Gerard Groote. Most historians have seen the movement as a reaction to the ecclesiastical and secular problems that dominated the times. At least three historians, Albert Hyma, Paul Mestwerdt, and G. Bonet-Maury, even see the New Devotion as fostering the rise of Humanism and, ultimately, of the Reformation: Both Erasmus and Martin Luther were schooled by those associated with the movement. Living in small, independent communities, the Brothers and Sisters of the Common Life, as they called themselves, strove to imitate the lives of the early Christians. They had little interest in philosophy, scholastic theology, or church politics; rather, through simplicity, humility and great faith they were intent on developing an intimate relationship with God and on nurturing a personal piety grounded in devotion to Jesus and to prayer and meditation.

Gerard Groote himself was born in 1340 in Deventer to a wealthy family. A bright young man, he entered the University of Paris at an early age and was a magister at 18, which brought him rich benefices, influence and luxury. But he found himself unsatisfied. Coming under the influence of Henry Egher of Calcar, Prior of the Carthusians at Monichuisen, he resigned his positions and spent three years with the Carthusians, seeking God's guidance for his life; then, with the approval of the Prior and the monks, he left Monichuisen to preach. His magnetic personality and his skill as an orator drew a large following, so much so that it aroused opposition from the local clergy, and the Bishop of Utrecht ordered him to stop. He did. Settling at Deventer, he directed his efforts to writing and to spiritual counseling. Again, though, he attracted a group of followers, and they formed the nucleus of the Brothers of the Common Life. Although not bound by permanent vows, they lived in poverty, chastity and obedience; held all property in common; and earned their own livelihood. They gained official approval by Pope St. Gregory XI in 1376. As the community grew and became more difficult to manage, Groote determined to place it under the direction and Rule of John Ruysbroeck, Prior of the Augustinian Canons Regular at Groenendaal. Before he could do so, however, he died of the Black Death in 1384, and Florens Radewijns, an early member of the Brothers, carried out his wishes. With the consent of the Bishop of Utrecht, a monastery was built at Windesheim in 1387. Then in 1389 a small community was set up on Mount St. Agnes under the direction of the Windesheim community; its first Prior was John Hemerken of Kampen, Thomas' older brother, and it is this community that Thomas entered, being formally accepted into the Congregation of the Canons Regular of St. Augustine on the feast of Corpus Christi, 1406.

Thomas played an active role in his monastery. His *Chronicle* tells us that he was elected Sub-Prior in 1425, when a Brother Theodoric became Prior, and we find him still holding that office in 1429. He probably resigned it when he left the community to attend to his dying brother, but we find him re-elected Sub-Prior again in 1448. He held the office for several years, for the next Sub-Prior mentioned is Henry Ruhorst, whose death is noted in 1458. During Thomas' tenure as Sub-Prior he also served as Novice Master, an important office in any monastery, for the Novice Master instructs young men during their formative years in the community. Thomas seems to have had a real gift for working with young people, for the unknown continuator of the *Chronicle* notes that "he composed various treatises for the edification of youth, unadorned and simple in style, but truly great in thought and efficacy," and he adds that Thomas "possessed a wonderful gift of consoling the tempted and afflicted." It was during his time as Novice Master that Thomas wrote his collection of sermons to the novices, and he probably wrote most of his other devotional works then, too, for they all clearly have a didactic purpose.

If Thomas wrote the *Imitation*, it was immediately before and during his first term as Novice Master, sometime between 1420 and 1427. Book 1 first appears in a manuscript dated 1424 and another appears dated 1425; all four books appear together in two dated manuscripts of 1427. The four books were written independently, each intended as a separate work: They were circulated separately; they appear in separate manuscripts; they do not carry a single title (the *Imitation of Christ* is the title of the first chapter of Book 1); and the four books appear in different sequences within manuscripts. The content of each book mirrors the content of Thomas' other devotional works, and each book reflects themes common to other writers of the New Devotion. But the *Imitation* stands to these other works as *Hamlet* stands to Shakespeare's other plays.

Although the four books were written as separate treatises, they have been read as a single book for five centuries; we have experienced the text as a whole, and we shall learn more from it if we read it and discuss it as a whole. In this regard, I agree with Professor Northrop Frye, who takes the same approach to reading and discussing the Bible. Like the *Imitation*, the Bible is a collection of independent books, but it too ''has traditionally been read as a unity, and has influenced Western imagination as a unity.'' The critical approach to works like the *Imitation* or the Bible ''begins with reading [them] straight through, as many times as may be necessary to possess [them] in totality. At that point the critic can begin to formulate a conceptual unity corresponding to the imaginative unity of his text.''[15]

If we read the *Imitation* straight through and not as four separate books, we shall discover a work that has no beginning, middle, or end, a work that is not linear as most works are. Even the Bible, a collection of many independent books, has an underlying linear structure: the creation of the world (Genesis), its salvation through Christ (the Gospels), and the end of the world (Revelation). But the *Imitation* does not. Rather than progressing in a straight line, the *Imitation* unfolds, gradually displaying the patterns of an intricate mosaic: Look closely and we shall see exquisitely crafted tiles; stand back a bit and dominant colors, subtle shadings and varied textures come to life; stand back further and the whole picture takes shape.

We have already examined one tile under a microscope—our *contemptus mundi* sentence. If we step back we shall see it blend into a deep swatch of color. When Thomas walked out of the world and into the monastery at Mount St. Agnes, his world seemed to be crumbling; ours might seem to be crumbling, too. As Ecclesiastes tells us, there is nothing new under the sun, nothing really changes. But Thomas did not enter the monastery to escape the world; he entered it to find God. True then, true now. A monastery provides a special environment in which a person gives himself entirely to God. Through prayer—serious, deep and abiding prayer—and through solitude, study, labor and penance, one strives to build an intimate relationship with God that reaches into the deepest recesses of the soul. It is a journey of wonder that touches something awesome and profound. And it is a journey that does not cut a person off from humankind, but one that joins him more intimately to it. Evagrius Ponticus, the fourth-century monk and mystical theologian, observed that "the monk is he who is separated from all and united in all."[16] St. Peter Damian echoes him in the 11th century by noting that "though we seem to be separated far from the Church through physical solitude, we are forever and most intimately in her presence"[17]; and in our own century, Vatican II firmly declares: "Let no one think that by their consecration religious have become strangers to their fellow men or useless citizens of this earthly city. For even though in some instances religious do not directly mingle with their contemporaries, yet in a more profound sense these same religious are united with them in the heart of Christ and cooperate with them spiritually."[18]

Thomas Merton, who entered the Trappist monastery of Our Lady of Gethsemani in Kentucky on December 10, 1941, three days after the Japanese attack on Pearl Harbor, vividly expressed this idea of the monk at the heart of the world when he first saw Gethsemani. The world had already passed through one world war, and it tottered on the brink of another when Merton arrived in the middle of the night as a visitor on April 7, 1941. As he approached the monastery, the tower, steeple and cross that used to crown the church glistened in the moonlight; he passed beneath the gatehouse arch and the words *Pax Intrantibus*; the guestmaster led him across the courtyard to a huge stone building with dark and silent windows; above a heavy door he saw the words *God*

Alone; and in his room the deep, deep silence of the night embraced him:

> This is the center of America. I had wondered what
> was holding the country together, what has been keeping
> the universe from cracking in pieces and falling apart. It is
> places like this monastery—not only this one: there must
> be others.
>
> Abraham prayed to the Lord to spare Sodom if there
> should be found in it ten just men. The Blessed Mother of
> God, the Queen of Heaven and of the Angels, shows Him
> daily her sons here, and because of their prayers the world
> is spared, from minute to minute....[19]

As Thomas à Kempis' world seemed to be crumbling in 1399, so did Merton's in 1941. Thomas confronted the Great Schism, the Black Death and massive social unrest; Merton saw grinding poverty and vicious hatred in Harlem as a graduate student at Columbia University, and then the world at war for a second time in 25 years. We, too, have seen our share of catastrophes: the genocide of our spiritual brothers and sisters, the Jews; war in Korea and Vietnam; genocide in Cambodia; famine in Ethiopia; AIDS; and the insane buildup of nuclear weapons that could instantly reduce God's earth to a smoking cinder wobbling in space. In 1978 the historian Barbara Tuchman wrote *A Distant Mirror: the Calamitous Fourteenth Century*, in which she suggests parallels between Thomas à Kempis' world and ours. It is a compelling thesis: In both worlds—if we listen carefully—we might imagine that we hear squeaking axles as chariots of fire pull into line for Armageddon.

One response to the sound is to wheel and deal and survive; another response is to pray. Thomas à Kempis chose the latter; so did Thomas Merton; so might we. When the *Imitation* advises us to separate ourselves from the world, we should not do so out of contempt for it, but out of a deep, unutterable love. The *Imitation of Christ* is a guidebook to a life of holiness whose end is God; the context in which we make the journey is the limited span of our earthly life, our ''seventy years or eighty for those who are strong.'' Given such a brief time, we might do well to focus on the fundamentals of our relationship with God and to ignore the distractions that the world sets in our path. We might begin by striving to achieve inner harmony, peace and quiet in our soul; "prepare the room for God to enter," as Thomas tells us. We each do so in our own way. A monk, in the 15th century or now, directs all his energy, thought and prayer to preparing a room for God; it is his sole occupation, the focus of his life. It is his contribution toward rebuilding God's world on a foundation of love; though separated from it, he is intensely part of it. Others of us may participate more actively in the world, but we too should strive above all else to place God at the center of our lives. Following Jesus' example, we might teach and heal and rebuild our world during the day, but at night we should retreat into the quiet of our own hearts for deep, intimate prayer; with God at the center, all we do will flow from him, and all we do will be for love of him.

So runs one dominant color in the mosaic. Others abound, as well. As we have examined the *contemptus mundi* theme, we could also examine the *Imitation*'s treatment of self, of friendship, of silence, of sin, and so on—all difficult topics requiring a deep exploration of historical, theological and linguistic context, if we are to respond to them as informed readers. Perhaps now, though, we should put such detailed examination aside for the moment, step back, and see the whole picture that sits before us. Tiles and colors can be fascinating in themselves, but it is in the mosaic as a whole that we experience its full meaning. As we step back, the picture takes shape: A person stands before God, profoundly alone; God embraces him with a deep and unutterable love; and with great humility he strives to love God in return. All else comes second; all else fades to metaphor and simile. It is this picture, and the exquisite simplicity and beauty with which it is crafted, that accounts for the *Imitation*'s thousands of editions and millions of readers over the last half a millenium. For in this picture we each see our own image. And as we ponder the lines of our own face, we understand as clearly as can be, why the *Imitation* should be picked up, dusted off, and read once again.

NOTES

1. *Boswell's Life of Johnson*, ed. by George Birbeck Hill, rev. by L.F. Powell, 6 vols. (Oxford: Clarendon Press, 1934), 3: 226.

2. George Birbeck Hill, ed., Johnsonian Miscellanies, 2 vols. (Oxford: Clarendon Press, 1897), 2: 153-154.

3. *The Collected Letters of Thomas and Jane Welsh Caryle*, ed. by Charles Richard Sanders and Kenneth J. Fielding, 9 vols. to date (Durham: Duke University Press, 1970 —), 6: 323.

4. *The George Eliot Letters*, ed. by Gordon S. Haight, 9 vols. (New Haven: Yale University Press, 1954-1978), 1: 278.

5. *The Mill on the Floss*, 3 vols. (Edinburgh: William Blackwood and Sons, 1860), 2: 186-187.

6. *The Collected Writings of Thomas de Quincey*, ed. by David Masson, 14 vols. (Edinburgh: Adam and Charles Block, 1889), 1: 5-6

7. "Marcus Aurelius," *The Complete Prose Works of Matthew Arnold*, ed. by R.H. Super, 11 vols. (Ann Arbor: The University of Michigan Press, 1960-1977), 3: 133.

8. *The Letters and Private Papers of William Makepeace Thackeray*, ed. by Gordon N. Ray, 4 vols. (Cambridge: Harvard University Press, 1946), 2: 616.

9. "Pastoral Constitution on the Church in the Modern World" (Vatican II, *Gaudium et Spes*, 7 December, 1965) in *Vatican Council II: the Conciliar and Post Conciliar Documents*, ed. by Austin Flannery, O.P., 2 vols. (Northport, NY: Costello Publishing Company, 1984), 1: 927; 904.

10. Book 1, Chapter 5.

11. One of the bibles is in the library of Darmstadt; the other is in Utrecht.

12. M.J. Pohl has edited Thomas' complete works in Latin. See *Thomae Hemerken a Kempis, Opera omnia*, 7 vols. (Friberg, 1902-1922).

13. Professor Fish first explored reader response in "Literature in the Reader: Affective Stylistics," *New Literary History* 2 (Autumn, 1970), 123-162.

14. Seneca says it in *Ad Lucilium Epistulae Morales*, 7: 3-4, Thomas, in the *Imitation*, Book 1, Chapter 20.

15. *The Great Code: the Bible and Literature*, (New York: Harcourt Brace Jovanovich, 1982), xii-xiii.

16. *De Oratione*, 124.

17. *Opusculi* XI, L. *qui appellatur Dominus vobiscum*, 10, *ML* 145, 239.

18. *Lumen gentium*, n. 46.

19. *Secular Journal* (New York: Farrar, Straus & Giroux, 1959), 183.

BOOK 1

*Useful Reminders
for the Spiritual Life*

Chapter 1

Of the Imitation of Christ

"Anyone who follows me shall not walk in darkness," says the Lord. These are the words of Christ, and by them we are reminded that we must imitate his life and his ways if we are to be truly enlightened and set free from the darkness of our own hearts. Let it be the most important thing we do, then, to reflect on the life of Jesus Christ.

Christ's teaching surpasses all the teachings of the saints, and the person who has his spirit will find hidden nourishment in his words. Yet, many people, even after hearing scripture read so often, lack a deep longing for it, for they do not have the spirit of Christ. Anyone who wishes to understand Christ's words and to savor them fully should strive to become like him in every way.

What good does it do, then, to debate about the Trinity, if by a lack of humility you are displeasing to the Trinity? In truth, lofty words do not make a person holy and just, but a virtuous life makes one dear to God. I would much rather feel profound sorrow for my sins than be able to define the theological term for it. If you knew the whole Bible by heart and the sayings of all the philosophers, what good would it all be without God's love and grace? Vanity of vanities and all is vanity, except to love God and to serve only him. This is the highest wisdom: to see the world as it truly is, fallen and fleeting; to love the world not for its own sake, but for God's; and to direct all your effort toward achieving the kingdom of heaven.

So, it is vanity to seek material wealth that cannot last and to place your trust in it. It is also vanity to seek recognition and status. It is vanity to chase after what the world says you should want and to long for things you should not have, things that you will pay a high price for later on if you get them. It is vanity to wish for a long life and to care little about a good life. It is vanity to focus only on your present life and not to look ahead to your future life. It is vanity to live for the joys of the moment and not to seek eagerly the lasting joys that await you.

Often remember that saying: "The eye is not satisfied with seeing, nor is the ear filled with hearing." Make every effort, then, to shift your affections from the things that you can see to the things you cannot see, for people who live in the world on its terms instead of on God's stain their conscience and lose God's grace.

Chapter 2

Of Having a Humble Opinion about Yourself

Everyone naturally wishes to have knowledge, but what good is great learning unless it is accompanied by a feeling of deep awe and profound reverence toward God? Indeed, a humble farmer who serves God is better than a proud philosopher, who, neglecting himself, contemplates the course of the heavens. The person who truly knows himself seems common in his own eyes, and the good things that others may say about him do not change the way he thinks about himself. If I knew everything in the world and did not have love, what good would it do me before God, who will judge me by what I have done?

Calm that excessive thirst for knowledge, for there is great discord and deception in it. People who have great learning are often eager to appear wise, and they often wish others to recognize them as wise people. There are many things that you can know about, though, that are of little or no use to the soul, and a person is exceedingly foolish who reaches for anything that does not lead toward salvation. Endless reading and talk do not satisfy the soul, but a good life puts the mind at rest, and a clean conscience brings great confidence in God. The more you know and the better you know it, the greater is your responsibility for using your knowledge wisely.

So, do not think highly of yourself because of what you know about any art or science, but rather respect the knowledge that has been entrusted to you. If it seems to you that you know many things and that you are an expert in them, recognize nevertheless that there are many things that you do not know. Do not be high-minded, but admit your great ignorance. Why do you wish to think yourself better than others when you discover many people more learned and more practiced in God's ways than you are? If you want to learn something that will really help you, learn to see yourself as God sees you and not as you see yourself in the distorted mirror of your own self-importance. This is the greatest and most useful lesson we can learn: to know ourselves for what we truly are, to admit freely our weaknesses and failings, and to hold a humble opinion of ourselves because of them. Not to dwell on ourselves and always to think well and highly of others is great wisdom and perfection.

If you should see another person sin openly or commit some grave wrong, still you should not think yourself a better person by comparison, for you do not know how long you may remain in a good state. We are all frail, but think no one more frail than yourself.

Chapter 3

Of the Teaching of Truth

Happy is that person whom Truth itself teaches, not by figures of speech and eloquent language, but as it is itself. Our opinions and our understanding often lead us astray and offer us very little insight. What good is a brilliant argument about hidden and obscure matters when God does not judge us by our knowledge of such things? It is a great mistake for us to neglect useful and necessary things and to direct our thoughts to curious and harmful ones. Having eyes, we do not see. Why should we bother about clever arguments and subtle reasoning?

When the eternal Word speaks we are set free from countless theories and conjectures. All things spring from this one Word and all things speak of one Word, and this Word is the beginning, which also speaks to us. Without the Word, no one understands correctly or draws the right conclusions about anything. That person to whom all things are One and who draws all things to One and who sees all things in One may be steadfast in heart and rest peacefully in God.

O God, the Truth, make me one with you in endless love! I am often worn out by all that I read and hear; you are all that I want or desire. Let all teachers hold their peace. Let all creation be silent in your sight. You alone speak to me.

The more a person is at one with himself and inwardly undivided, the more varied and profound things does he understand without effort, for he receives the light of understanding from above. A pure, simple and steady spirit is not distracted by flitting about from one thing to another, for he does all things to the honor of God and tries in his heart to be free from all selfishness. What gets in your way and troubles you more than the undisciplined passions of your own heart? A good, devout person first arranges inwardly the things to be done outwardly. He does not let his passions get the best of him, but he subjects them to the ruling of sound judgment. Who has a more fierce struggle than the person who strives to master himself? And this must be our occupation: to strive to master ourselves and daily to grow stronger and to advance from good to b...

...n this life has some accompanying imperfection, and ... not without some darkening mist. A humble under... ...is a surer way to God than a profound searching ...vledge is not to be blamed, nor is the simple un... ...which is good in itself and which is made to be ...science and a virtuous life are always to be put ...people have chosen to seek knowledge rather ...are often led astray and their lives come to ...Oh, if they would apply such diligence in ...ng virtues as they do in posing questions, ...ils and scandals among people, nor so ...nities!

Sur... ...gment comes we shall not be asked what we... ...ve done, not how well we have spoken but ho... ...Tell me, where are those professors and tea... ...ew so well while they were living and flourishi... ...v other people hold their positions, and I do not know whether they ever think of them. While they lived they seemed to be important, and now no one mentions them. Oh, how swiftly the glory of the world passes away! If only their lives had been in harmony with their learning, then all their studying and reading would have been worthwhile. How many people perish in a generation through empty learning, caring little for the service of God? And because they prefer to be famous rather than humble, they perish with their own thoughts.

That person is truly great who has great love. He is truly great who is small in his own eyes and who regards every pinnacle of honor as nothing in itself. He is truly wise who regards all earthly ambitions as supremely unimportant, if they stand in the way of gaining Christ. And he is very learned indeed who knows God's will and who makes it his own.

Chapter 4

Of Thinking before You Act

We should not trust every word that we hear or every feeling in our hearts; rather, we should bring such matters before God and carefully ponder them at our leisure. It is sad to say, but we are so weak that we are more ready to believe bad things about another person—and to spread them around—than we are to believe or to say something good about them. Those who strive to be perfect, though, are not so quick to believe everything that is said, because they understand human weakness, which is prone to evil and is slippery enough in words.

It is great wisdom not to be rash in our actions nor to persist stubbornly in our own opinions. What is more, it is wise not to believe everything you hear nor to be so eager to pass on rumors. Instead of following your own notions, consult someone who is wise and conscientious, and seek to be guided by one who is better than yourself. A good life makes a person wise in God's eyes and experienced in many things. The more humble and obedient one is to God, the greater will be his wisdom and peace.

Chapter 5

Of Reading Holy Writings

Search for truth in holy writings, not eloquence. All holy writing should be read in the same spirit with which it was written. We should look for profit in the writings rather than for subtle expression. We should read devout and simple books as willingly as we read those that are lofty and profound. Do not let the writer's authority or learning influence you, be it little or great, but let the love of pure truth attract you to read. Do not ask, "Who said this?" but pay attention to what is said. People pass away, but the truth of the Lord endures forever. God speaks to us in many ways without considering a person's status.

Our curiosity often gets in our way when we try to study and understand those passages that are too difficult for us. We should simply pass over them. If you wish to profit from your reading, read with humility, simplicity and faith, and do not try to impress others with your great learning. Feel free to question, listen in silence to the words of the saints, and do not scoff at what the ancient writers have to say, for it is not offered without cause.

Chapter 6

Of Confused Feelings

Whenever a person becomes obsessed with success and material things, he quickly becomes restless. The proud and greedy never rest; the poor and humble in spirit rest in great peace. Anyone who is not completely free from the grip of his own vanity is easily tempted and is toppled by small, trifling things.

A person who is weak in spirit and who is still controlled by his need to be important has great trouble dragging himself away from the things that most attract him in this world. Such a person is unhappy when he does restrain himself, yet his anger flares up if anyone stands in his way. What is more, if he does get what he wants, he is at once stricken by a heavy conscience because he has given in to his weakness. In no way does this lead to peace!

In resisting such temptations, then, does one find true peace of heart, not in being a slave to them. There is no peace in the heart of a slave, nor in someone who is driven to continually bustling about in the world. Only a spiritual person—a person aglow with God's love—finds true peace.

Chapter 7

Of Avoiding Empty Hope and Self-Praise

Anyone who places all his trust in people or in other created things is foolish. Do not be ashamed to serve others for the love of Jesus Christ and to appear poor in this world. Do not rely on yourself, but place all your trust in God. Do what you can, and God will bless your good intentions. Do not trust in your own knowledge nor in anyone else's cleverness; rather, trust in the grace of God, who helps the humble and humbles the proud.

Do not take pride in your possessions, if you have any, nor in your friends because they are powerful and influential; instead, take pride in God who gives all things and who wishes to give himself above all. Do not brag about the size or beauty of your body, which a little sickness can spoil and disfigure. Do not be pleased with yourself about your ability or talent, lest you displease God, from whom comes the sum of whatever natural good you have. Do not think that you are better than others, lest you appear worse in God's eyes; God knows what we are. Do not be proud of your good deeds, for God's judgments differ from ours, and he is often displeased by what pleases us.

If you have any good qualities, believe that other people have better ones; by doing so you will retain your humility. It does you no harm if you place yourself beneath everyone else; it does you great harm, though, if you place yourself above even one other person. A person who is humble is always at peace, but a proud person carries a heart filled with envy and resentment.

Chapter 8

Of Avoiding Inappropriate Intimacy

Do not open your heart to everyone, but discuss your private concerns with a person who is wise and who reveres God. Do not spend much time with young people or strangers; instead, develop the friendships you have, especially with those who are older and wiser than you are. Do not flatter the rich, and do not be eager to be seen with important people. Rather, be with the humble and the simple, with the devout and the obedient, and talk about those things which help you to become more holy. If you are a man under religious vows, do not be intimate with any woman, but commend all good women in general to God; if you are a woman under religious vows, do likewise with men. Seek, instead, a more intimate friendship with God and his angels, and avoid becoming emotionally or spiritually dependent on other people.

We should have great love toward everyone, but intimacy often gets in the way of our spiritual development. Sometimes it happens that a stranger shines from a good reputation, but when we meet him he falls far short of what we expected. Sometimes we intend to please others by our own company, and instead we displease them by the shortcomings they see in us.

Chapter 9

Of Obedience for Those under Religious Vows

It is a very great thing for a person under religious vows to welcome obedience, to live under a Superior, and not to be independent; it is much safer to serve than to lead. Many people are under obedience more out of necessity than love, and there is no end to their unhappiness and complaining because of it. They will never gain spiritual freedom unless they wholeheartedly give up their freedom for the love of God. Run here or run there, you will find no peace except by humbly placing yourself under the rule of a Superior. Many people imagine that they will be better off in another monastery, but they are only fooling themselves.

It is true that we all wish to act as we please, and we all like those people best who agree with us. But if God is among us, it is sometimes necessary to give up our own way of thinking for the sake of peace. Who is so wise that he can understand everything? So, do not have too much confidence in your own opinion, but be willing to hear what others have to say. If your opinion is good and if you leave it for the love of God and follow someone else's, you will be a better person for it. Indeed, I have often heard that it is safer to hear and to accept advice than to give it. It may also happen that each person's opinion may be good, but to refuse to yield to others when reason or cause requires it is a sign of pride and stubbornness.

Chapter 10

f Avoiding Unnecessary Talk

As much as you can, avoid being caught up in day-to-day business, for spending too much energy on it gets in the way of our spiritual journey. Even if we have the best of intentions, it easily dominates our lives and we quickly become proud of our successes. I often wish that I had kept silent and had not been so quick to venture out into the world.

I wonder why are we so eager to chatter and gossip with each other, since we seldom return to the quiet of our own hearts without a damaged conscience? The reason is that by idle chit-chat we seek comfort from one another and we hope to lighten our distracted hearts. And to make matters worse, we chatter most freely about our favorite topics, about what we would like to have, or about those things we especially dislike!

What a mistake! This outside comfort is no small detriment to the inner comfort that comes from God. Therefore, we must watch and pray that we do not waste time. If it is proper to speak, speak of what will benefit others spiritually. Bad habits and neglect of our spiritual progress contribute much to our endless chatter; however, devout conversation on spiritual matters greatly helps our progress, particularly where people of like mind and spirit are bound to each other in God.

Chapter 11

Of Finding Peace and Making Spiritual Progress

We might have much peace if we were not such busy-bodies, for what others say and do is no concern of ours. How can anyone remain at peace for long who entangles himself in other people's business, who constantly seeks new things to do, or who is hardly ever at peace in his own heart? Blessed are the simple in heart, for they shall have much peace!

How were some of the saints so perfect and contemplative? They strove to subordinate all their earthly desires to heavenly ones, and by doing so they could cling to God from the very depths of their hearts and freely attend to him. We are too occupied with our own concerns and too interested in the passing affairs of the world. We seldom completely overcome a single fault, and we have little enthusiasm for our daily progress; thus, we remain cold and only vaguely interested in what we are doing. If we were not so absorbed in ourselves and if we were less confused in our own hearts, then we might savor divine things and experience something of heavenly contemplation. The greatest hindrance to our spiritual development—indeed, the whole hindrance—is that we allow our passions and desires to control us, and we do not strive to walk in the perfect way of the saints. When we meet the least adversity, we are too quickly dejected and we turn to other people for comfort, instead of to God.

If we made an effort to stand firmly and courageously in the struggle, doubtless we should see the help of our Lord from heaven, for he is ready to help those who trust in his grace; he gives us occasions to fight that we may win. If our spiritual progress relies only on outward observances, our devotion will not last long. Let us lay the axe to the root, so that being purged of unruly passions we may have peace of mind.

If every year we uprooted a single fault, we should soon become perfect. But we often feel that we were better and more pure at the beginning of our spiritual lives than we are now after many years of living our vows! Fervor and progress ought to increase daily, but it is thought to be a fine thing these days if a person can hold on to even a little of those first intense feelings! If we would exercise a little self-discipline at the beginning, then we would later be able to do everything easily and joyfully.

It is hard to give up old habits, but it is even harder to go against one's own will. Yet, if you cannot overcome small, trivial things, when will you overcome difficult ones? Fight the urge when it starts, and break off bad habits, lest perhaps, little by little, they lead you into greater trouble. Oh, if you could only know how much peace for yourself and joy for others your good efforts could bring, I think you would be more anxious for spiritual growth!

Chapter 12

Of Putting Troubles to Use

Sometimes it is good for us to have troubles and hardships, for they often call us back to our own hearts. Once there, we know ourselves to be strangers in this world, and we know that we may not believe in anything that it has to offer. Sometimes it is good that we put up with people speaking against us, and sometimes it is good that we be thought of as bad and flawed, even when we do good things and have good intentions. Such troubles are often aids to humility, and they protect us from pride. Indeed, we are sometimes better at seeking God when people have nothing but bad things to say about us and when they refuse to give us credit for the good things we have done! That being the case, we should so root ourselves in God that we do not need to look for comfort anywhere else.

When a person of good will is troubled or tempted or vexed by evil thoughts, then he better understands his need for God, without whom he can do nothing good at all. In such a state, he is sad and he sighs and prays because of the miseries he suffers; then, he is tired of living any longer and he wishes to die, so that he may be set free to be with Christ. When all that happens, he knows for certain that perfect security and full peace cannot exist in this world.

Chapter 13

Of Resisting Temptations

As long as we live in this world we cannot be without trials and temptations; hence, it is written in Job: "Our life on earth is a temptation." We should be anxious, then, about our temptations and be watchful in prayer, lest the devil, who never sleeps but prowls around seeking whom he may devour, find room to trick us.

No one is so perfect and so holy that he does not sometimes have temptations; we cannot be without them entirely. Yet, temptations are often very good for a person, granted that they are troublesome and unpleasant, for through them one is humbled, cleansed and instructed. All the saints have passed through many trials and temptations and have profited from them. Those who could not deal with temptations have become lost and have fallen away.

There is no religious order so holy nor place so secluded that there are no temptations or hardships. No one is entirely safe from temptation no matter how long he lives, for we carry temptation's source within us: We have all been born with a fierce, self-centered desire for success, status and pleasure that clashes with our longing for God. When one temptation or trial is over, another comes along, and we shall always have something to contend with, for we have lost the original happiness that God intended for us. Many people try to escape temptations, then fall more severely into them! We cannot win by running away, but by patience and true humility we become stronger than all our enemies.

The person who only runs away from temptation and does not tear it out by the root will not gain very much. In fact, for such a person, temptations will quickly return, and they will be even worse. If you patiently put up with them, you will gradually overcome your temptations better through God's grace than by your own harshness and self-assertion. When you are tempted, seek advice often, and never deal harshly with others who are tempted; instead, comfort them as you would have them comfort you.

The beginning of all evil temptations is a mind not firmly fixed on its purpose and a small trust in God, for as a ship without a rudder is driven to and fro by the waves, so a careless person who abandons his course is tempted in many ways. Fire tempers iron, and temptation tempers the just person. Often, we do not know what we are able to do, but temptation reveals what we are. One must be watchful, however, especially when temptation begins, for then the enemy is more easily overcome if he is not allowed to enter inside the mind's door but is kept firmly outside the threshold while he knocks. It is for this reason that someone said: "Resist the beginning; the remedy comes too late," for first a simple thought comes to the mind, and then a vivid picture takes shape; afterward comes delight, then a small mental concession, and finally ready acceptance. Thus, little by little, the malignant enemy gains full entrance when he is not resisted at the beginning. And the longer one puts off resisting, the weaker he becomes each day and the stronger the enemy grows.

Some people suffer terrible temptations at the beginning of their lives with Christ. Some at the end. And some suffer their entire lives. Some people are tempted lightly enough, and this is according to God's wisdom and fairness. God ponders the state and merits of all people, and he arranges everything in advance for our well-being. So, we must not despair when tempted, but pray to God the more fervently that he may see fit to help us. Certainly God, accordingly to the saying of Paul, "will make such issue with temptation that we may be able to bear it." So, let us humble our souls under God's hand in every temptation and trouble, for he will save the humble in spirit and raise them up.

By temptations and troubles a person proves how much progress he has made in the spiritual life, and in that stands great merit and virtue shines more clearly. It is no great thing if a person is devout and eager for holiness when he feels no burden, but if he endures patiently during difficult times, there is hope of great progress. Some people are spared from great temptations and are often overcome in small daily ones. This happens so that, being humbled, they may never trust themselves in great things if they are so weak in such ordinary ones.

Chapter 14

Of Avoiding Hasty Judgments

Look to yourself, and beware of judging what others do. In judging others a person works to no purpose, often makes mistakes, and easily does the wrong thing, but in judging and analyzing ourselves, we always work to our own advantage.

Our judgments are often based on our personal likes and dislikes; consequently, our private prejudices can easily overshadow our sound thinking. If we would always have our attention focused on God and if we would long for him alone, we would not be so easily upset when others do not accept what we have to say. But often something lurks within us, or intrudes from outside of us, which draws us along with it. Many people have their own private motives for what they do, and they are not even aware of them. They seem to be quite content when things are done as they like, but if events take a different turn, they quickly become testy and withdrawn. Differences of thought and opinion lead to more than enough bickering among friends and neighbors, among religious and devout people.

Old habits are hard to break, and no one is easily led beyond his own point of view. If you lean more on your own reason or diligence than on the strength of your life with Jesus Christ, you will have only a slim chance of becoming an enlightened person—and if you do, it will happen slowly, indeed. God wants us to conform our lives perfectly to his will and to reach beyond our passions and prejudices through an intense love for him.

Chapter 15

Of Works Done Out of Love

Never do what you know is wrong for anything in the world or to please anyone. Yet, to serve the needy a good work may be put aside or exchanged for a better one. In doing so, a good work is not lost; it is changed into something better.

Without love good works are worthless, but with love they become wholly rewarding no matter how small and insignificant they may seem. Indeed, God places more importance on the reason you work than on how much work you actually do. A person does much who loves much; he does much who does it well; he does well who serves the common good rather than himself.

Often what seems to be love is not love at all but the natural feelings that we all have. Along with such feelings, though, usually come questionable motives, such as willfulness, the hope of reward and self-interest. The person who has pure and perfect love, however, seeks self-praise in nothing, but wishes only that God may be glorified in everything. Such a person envies no one, for he sees God in everyone. He does not wish to take pleasure in himself, but he wishes to become blessed in God's eyes above all good things. He believes that God is the source of everything; like a spring, all good flows from him. In the end, all the saints come to rest in God. Oh, a person who has even a spark of real love should truly feel all the things of this world to be of little importance, compared to God!

Chapter 16

Of Putting Up with Others' Faults

What we cannot change in ourselves or in others we ought to endure patiently until God wishes it to be otherwise. Perhaps it is this way to try our patience, for without trials our merits count for little. Nevertheless, when you run into such problems you ought to pray that God may find it fitting to help you and that you may bear your troubles well. If anyone who is spoken to once or twice will not listen and change his ways, do not argue with him, but leave it all to God, for he knows well how to turn bad things into good. He knows how to accomplish his will and how to express himself fully in all his servants.

Take pains to be patient in bearing the faults and weaknesses of others, for you too have many flaws that others must put up with. If you cannot make yourself as you would like to be, how can you expect to have another person entirely to your liking? We would willingly have others be perfect, and yet we fail to correct our own faults. We want others to be strictly corrected, and yet we are unwilling to be corrected ourselves. Other peoples' far-ranging freedom annoys us, and yet we insist on having our own way. We wish others to be tied down by rules, and yet we will not allow ourselves to be held in check in any way at all. It is evident how rarely we think of our neighbor as ourselves!

If everything were perfect, what would we have to endure from others for God's sake? But now God has so arranged things that we may learn to bear each other's burdens, for no one is without faults, no one is without burdens, no one is wholly self-sufficient, no one has enough wisdom all by himself. That being the case, we must support and comfort each other; together we must help, teach and advise one another, for the strength that each person has will best be seen in times of trouble. Such times do not make us weak; they show what we are.

Chapter 17

Of the Monastic Life

You should learn to discipline yourself in many things if you wish to keep peace and harmony with others. It is no small thing to live in a monastery or a religious community and to remain there without complaining and to persevere faithfully until death. Blessed is that person who has lived there well and has finished happily! If you wish to act as you should, and if you wish to make progress, think of yourself as a stranger on earth, as a pilgrim. You should become a fool for Christ if you wish to lead a religious life. What you wear and the customs you follow contribute little; rather, changing your ways and refocusing all of your energies toward the spiritual life will make you a true religious.

A person who seeks anything other than the purely divine and the well-being of his soul will find nothing but trouble and sorrow in a monastery. Likewise, one cannot remain at peace for long who does not strive to be the least important person in the community, attending to others with humility and love. You have come to serve, not to rule. Know that you are called to endurance and work, not to idleness and talk. In the monastery, a person is tried like gold in the furnace; here, no one can stay unless he resolves wholeheartedly to live a humble life for God.

Chapter 18

Of the Examples of the Holy Fathers

Look into the lively examples of the holy fathers, in whom true perfection and religion shone, and you will see that what we do is very little—indeed, it is almost nothing. Alas! what is our life if compared with theirs? Saints and friends of Christ, they served the Lord in hunger and thirst, in cold and nakedness, in toil and weariness, in vigils and fasts, in prayers and holy meditations, in persecutions and in many scornful insults. Oh, how many grave troubles they suffered, the apostles, martyrs, confessors, virgins and all the others who resolved to follow Christ! They did not care about their lives in this world, as long as they might possess them in eternal life.

Oh, how strict and renounced a life the holy fathers led in the desert; what long and heavy temptations they endured; how often they were harassed by the enemy; how many passionate prayers they offered to God; what rigorous abstinence they practiced; what great zeal and fervor they had for spiritual growth; what courageous struggles they waged to overcome their weaknesses; what pure and upright efforts they continually made toward God!

They labored throughout the day and at night they were free for long hours of prayer, although during work they did not cease at all from mental prayer. They spent all their time profitably. Every hour free to attend to God seemed short, and in the great sweetness of contemplation they sometimes completely forgot to take care of their physical needs! They gave up all riches, dignities, honors, friends and relatives; they clung to nothing of this world. They scarcely would take the necessities of life: Diverting their attention from God to themselves, even when they had to, pained them. So, they were poor in earthly things but very rich in grace and virtue. Outwardly they were in want, but inwardly they were refreshed with God's grace and comfort.

The world saw them as strangers, but God saw them as close and intimate friends. To themselves they seemed insignificant. The world often despised them, but in God's eyes they were precious and beloved. They were grounded in true humility; they lived in simple obedience; they walked in love and patience; and so they grew daily in spirit, and they won great grace with God. They are given as examples for all of us, and they ought to challenge us more to progress well than a legion of apathetic people tempt us to relax.

Oh, how great was the fervor of all religious men and women in the early days of their holy orders! Oh, how great was their devotion in prayer, and how great was their rivalry in virtue! What great discipline they had, and what reverence and obedience blossomed in them all under the rule of a Superior! The traces left even now speak to the fact that they were truly holy and perfect people, who, fighting vigorously, rose above all the temptations of this world.

In these days a person is thought to be great who stays out of trouble and who patiently accepts what he has undertaken! Ah, the indifference and negligence of the way things are today! Nowadays we quickly fall away from our first intense spiritual feelings, and out of weariness and indifference we soon grow tired of living! Oh, that the desire to grow in virtue may not sleep in you when you have often seen so many examples of such great devotion!

Chapter 19

Of the Training of a Good Religious Person

The life of a good, religious person ought to be strong in every virtue so that he may truly be what others think him to be. And he should be so with good reason, for it is God who watches us—God, whom we ought to revere wherever we are, and walk the world as pure as angels in his sight. Every day we should renew our resolve to live a holy life, and everyday we should kindle ourselves to a burning love, just as if today were the first day of our new life in Christ. We should say: "Help me, Lord God, to fulfill my good intention and your holy service. Starting today, let me begin perfectly, for what I have done so far is nothing."

Progress follows intention, and a person needs much earnest effort if he wishes to progress well, for if someone who resolutely plans often fails, what will happen to the person who seldom plans anything and who cannot carry out his plans even when he makes them? Many things may cause us to walk away from what we have started, and we seldom do so without some loss. The intention of earnest and well-meaning people depends more on the grace of God than on their own wisdom; such people always place their trust in God no matter what they do, for man proposes but God disposes. The path a person takes does not lie within himself.

If for piety's sake or another person's benefit we sometimes skip a spiritual exercise that we are used to doing, it may be made up easily later on. But if we skip it out of boredom or negligence, it is a real fault and will prove harmful. Try as we may, it is still easy to fall short in many things. Nevertheless, we should always have some definite plan firmly in mind, especially one to counter those things which most often stand in our way. We must examine our outward and inward affairs and set them both in order, for both are necessary for our spiritual progress.

If you cannot be at one with yourself all the time, try to be so at least once a day, particularly in the morning or evening. In the morning make your plans; in the evening go over your conduct, reviewing how you behaved this day in word, deed and thought, for in these you may often have displeased God or your neighbor. Arm yourself courageously against the devil's reckless arrogance. Curb your appetite and you will have an easier time restraining yourself from a whole list of other cravings. Never be completely idle, but be reading or writing or praying or meditating or working in some way for the common good.

For all that, physical disciplines are to be undertaken with discretion, and they are not to be taken up equally by everyone. Those practices which are not part of community life are not to be displayed in public, for private things are more safely worked at alone. Take care not to be sluggish toward common practices and more enthusiastic toward private ones, but once you have fully and faithfully fulfilled what you ought to do, if you have free time, then you may give yourself to your private devotions. All people cannot have the same disciplines, but this is more proper for one, that for another.

Moreover, for certain times different disciplines are appropriate; some are appropriate for feast days, others are more fitting for common days. Some we need in time of temptation and others in time of peace and quiet. Some we love to think of when we are sad and others when we are joyful in the Lord. Around principal feasts we should renew good disciplines and more fervently ask the saints for their prayers. From feast to feast we should resolve to live as if we were about to leave this world and come to the eternal feast; therefore, we should prepare ourselves carefully at times of devotion, live more devoutly, and keep every observance more strictly, as if shortly God were to reward us for our labor. And if our reward is delayed, let us believe ourselves the less well prepared, still unworthy of the glory that shall be revealed to us at the proper time. Let us be eager to prepare ourselves better for our departure. "Blessed is the servant," says Luke the Evangelist, "whom the Lord, when he comes, will find on guard. In truth I say to you, he will set him over all that he has."

Chapter 20

Of the Love of Solitude and Silence

Seek a proper time to be at leisure with yourself, and think often of God's kindness. Leave curiosity alone. Read subjects that touch the heart rather than those that pass the time. If you will avoid needless talk and idle visits and not listen for the latest gossip, you will find plenty of suitable time for good meditations. The greatest saints guarded their time alone and chose to serve God in solitude. Someone has said, "As often as I went out among men, I returned less of a man." We often experience this when we have spent a long time in idle chatter. It is easier to be completely silent than not to be long-winded; it is easier to stay at home than to be properly on guard outside the monastery. A person whose goal is the inward, spiritual life must cast his lot with Jesus and not follow the crowd.

No one is secure except the person who freely keeps to himself. No one speaks securely except the person who willingly keeps silent. No one leads securely except the person who freely serves. No one commands securely except the person who thoroughly obeys. No one knows secure joy except the person who holds a good conscience in his own heart.

The security of the saints always sprang from holding God in deep awe and profound reverence. And just because their great virtues and grace were so evident did not mean that they no longer had to be diligent and humble. The assurance of lesser people springs from pride and presumption; in the end it becomes self-deception. Whether you are a good monk or a devout hermit, never promise yourself security in this life. Often those people whom others hold in the highest esteem have been placed in serious danger by their own overconfidence. So, it is better for many people that they not be entirely free from temptation. Rather, they should be attacked by it often, lest they become overconfident or puffed with pride or attracted to material comforts instead of to God.

Oh, if we never sought after fleeting joys or never busied ourselves chasing after possessions and status, what a good conscience we would keep! Oh, if we would get rid of all empty cares and think only on wholesome and divine things and place all our hope in God, what great peace and rest we would have! No one is worthy of heavenly comfort unless he has spent great effort training himself in true sorrow for his own failings and in deep compassion for others.

If you wish to feel this in your heart, go into your room and shut out the noise of the world. As it is written: "In the privacy of your room, feel sorrow and compassion deeply." In your room you will find what you often let slip outside. A room continually used grows sweet; ill-kept it breeds boredom. If you stay in your room and keep it well when you first turn to God, then later on it will become a beloved friend and a dear comfort.

In silence and peace a devout soul makes progress and learns the secrets of the scriptures. Only in silence and peace does a devout soul find floods of tears in which it may wash and cleanse itself each night. The further the soul is from the noise of the world, the closer it may be to its Creator, for God, with his holy angels, will draw close to a person who seeks solitude and silence. It is better to remain alone and to care for your soul than to neglect yourself and work miracles. It is praiseworthy for a person under monastic vows to stay in his monastery, to avoid being seen, and to keep to himself. Why wish to see what you cannot have? The world passes away and so does the craving for what it has to offer. The desire to see, to hear, to smell, to taste and to touch all those things that you do without will lead you astray. Then, after you indulge your desires, what will you carry back to the monastery but a heavy conscience and a divided heart? A happy outing often brings a sad return, and a happy evening makes an unhappy morning. All such joys enter delightfully in just this way, but in the end they bite and destroy.

What can you see elsewhere that you cannot see here? Look at the sky and earth and all the elements, for from these all things are made. What can you see anywhere under the sun that can endure for long? Perhaps you think to satisfy yourself? Forget it. You cannot. If you could see all things at once right in front of your eyes, what would it all be but an empty vision? Lift your eyes to God on high, and pray for what you have done and for what you have failed to do. Leave vain things to vain people, and give your attention to those things that God asks of you. Go into your room, shut your door, and call upon Jesus, your Beloved. Stay with him in the privacy of your own room, for you will not find such peace anywhere else. If you had not gone out simply to amuse yourself or if you had not listened so readily to this or that bit of gossip, you would have continued on in true peace better than you have. If you like to do such things, then afterwards you have to put up with a restless heart.

Chapter 21

Of Heartfelt Remorse

If you wish to make any spiritual progress, keep yourself rooted in a profound love of God; do not be too free, but direct all your feelings toward maintaining an inner calm, and do not cave in to chasing after empty pleasures. Regret your sins from the bottom of your heart, and you will find true devotion. Remorse opens up many good things which laxity is usually quick to ruin. It is a wonder that a person can ever completely rejoice in this life if he reflects on how far he has strayed from God and on the many dangers to his soul.

Through a light heart and indifference to our faults, we fail to feel the sorrows of our souls; indeed, we often laugh when we should weep. There is no true freedom nor real joy except in loving God and in having a good conscience. That person is indeed fortunate who can throw off all distractions that get in his way and who can focus intently on feeling deep sorrow for his sins. The person who separates himself from whatever can stain or burden his conscience is truly happy. Fight bravely, for habit overcomes habit. If you can leave others alone, they will gladly let you do what you have to do. Do not be drawn into other people's affairs nor entangle yourself with the concerns of people in high places. Always keep an eye on yourself first, and take special care to correct yourself before correcting your friends. If people do not like you, do not be sad about it. But do be sad about this: that you do not live as well and as carefully as a servant of God and a devout, religious person should.

It is often more useful and safer not to have many comforts in this life, especially physical comforts. Yet, if we lack comforts from God, or if we do not feel them very often, it is our own fault, for we rarely take the time to recognize our sins and to feel sorrow for them. When we do, we are sure to feel unworthy of God's favor and more worthy of the estrangement that we do feel. When a person becomes filled with sorrow and regret for his sins, then the whole world looks different to him. A good person finds reason enough for mourning and weeping, for whether he thinks of himself or of his neighbor, he knows that no one lives without hardships in this life. And the more closely he examines himself the more he grieves. The grounds for our just grief and remorse are our faults and our sins. We lie so entangled in them that we are seldom able to fix our minds on heavenly things.

If you thought more often of your death than of a long life, you would doubtless correct yourself more earnestly. And if you would prudently consider the future punishment of hell or purgatory, I believe that you would freely bear labor and sorrow and would not be afraid to go to great extremes to be worthy of God's grace. But because these things do not cut through to our hearts, and because we still cling to those things that flatter us, we remain cold and terribly lazy. Often it is a lack of spirit that makes us so willing to complain; therefore, humbly pray to the

Lord that he may help you feel sorrow for your sins, and say with the prophet: "Feed me, Lord, with the bread of tears, and give me a measure of tears to drink."

Chapter 22

Of Human Misery

You are unhappy wherever you are and wherever you turn unless you turn yourself to God. Why are you troubled because things do not work out the way you would like? Is there anyone who has everything he wants? I don't. You don't. No one on earth does. There is no one in the world without some trouble or uncertainty, be he a king or a pope. Who is it who has the better part? Certainly, the person who can endure anything for God.

Many people who do not know any better say, "See what a good life that man has! How rich, how great, how powerful and distinguished!" But direct your attention toward heavenly riches and you will see that all these possessions and honors are awfully flimsy; even more, they are oppressive, because a person never has them without anxiety and fear. A person's happiness is not in having many possessions; indeed, a modest share is enough.

Truly, life can be a great trial! The more one wishes to be spiritual, the more difficult the present life can seem, for as one progresses in the spiritual life, his flawed nature becomes more and more apparent. To eat, to drink, to watch, to sleep, to rest, to work and to be subject to life's other necessities can be a great bother to a devout person who wishes to concentrate on the spiritual life. Indeed, a person who quietly lives his life in his own heart is greatly weighed down by what the world requires of him; whence, the prophet devoutly prays that he may be freed as far as possible, saying: "Deliver me from my necessities, Lord."

But woe to them who do not know the true state of their own souls, and more woe to them who prize this unhappy, flawed life as the highest good. Some people cling so tightly to life that, although they can scarcely get the bare necessities by working or begging, they would still be willing to live here forever, caring nothing for the kingdom of God. Oh, how mad and faithless in heart are such people, who lie so deeply mired in their own immediate concerns that they care for nothing but material things! And, indeed, in the end these unfortunate people will know to their sorrow how cheap and worthless were those things that were so important to them. On the other hand, God's saints and all the devout friends of Christ took no account of material possessions nor of what marked success in this life, but their whole hope and intent focused on eternal possessions. All that they wished for was lifted up toward the permanent and invisible, lest love of visible things should drag them down to the lowest depths.

My dear friend, do not lose confidence in progressing in the spiritual life; you still have time and opportunity. Why put off your decision? Get up and begin at once and say: "Now is the time to act. Now is the time to fight. Now is the proper time to change." When you are out of sorts and troubled, then is the time for gaining merit. You must go through fire and water before you come to comfort. Unless you discipline yourself rigorously, you will not overcome your weaknesses. As long as we carry about this frail body, we cannot be free of sin nor can we live without weariness and sorrow. We would willingly be at rest from all trouble, but because we have lost our innocence through sin, we have also lost our true happiness; therefore, you must have patience and wait for God's mercy until this difficulty passes and death is swallowed up by life.

Oh, how great is human frailty, which is always prone to doing those things it shouldn't! Today you confess your sins and tomorrow you do what you confessed all over again! Now you resolve to be on guard and an hour later you act as if you had never made the decision! Since we are so frail and unstable, we are right in having a humble opinion of ourselves. We can quickly lose through carelessness what we gained through grace with much time and effort.

What will become of us in the end, we who so quickly lose our resolve? Too bad for us if we wish to settle back and rest as if peace and safety were already accomplished! Why, not a sign of true holiness has yet to appear in our daily lives! It would be good for us to start all over and, like good beginners, be taught the ways of good behavior once again. If we did, there might be some hope of changing in the future and some hope of spiritual progress.

Chapter 23

Of Thinking about Death

Very soon it will be over with you here; then, see how things stand! Today we are, and tomorrow we are gone. And when we are taken out of sight, we soon pass out of mind. Oh, the dullness and hardness of our hearts that only think of the present and do not look forward more to the future. This being the case, you ought to master yourself in every act and thought as if you were to die today. If you had a good conscience, you would not fear death so much. It would be better to guard against sins than to run away from death. If you are not prepared today, how will you be ready tomorrow? Tomorrow is an uncertain day, and how do you know if you will have a tomorrow?

What good is it to live long when we improve so little? A long life does not always improve us; in fact, it often adds to our problems! Would that we could spend even one day well in this world! Many people count the years of their lives in Christ, but often not much comes of their attempts to change their lives. If it is frightful to die, perhaps it is more dangerous still to live a long life. Blessed is that person who always has the hour of death before his eyes and who is daily prepared to die!

If you have ever seen a person die, reflect that you too must pass the same way. When it is morning, imagine that you may not reach evening. But, when evening is done, do not be so bold as to promise yourself a morning. Always be ready, therefore, and live so that death may never find you unprepared. Many people die suddenly and unexpectedly; no one knows at what hour the Son of Man will come. When that final hour does come, you will begin to think quite differently about all your past life, and you will be exceedingly sorry that you were so careless and remiss.

How happy and wise is that person who strives now to be in life what he wishes to be found in death. He will die happily if he has lived for God and not for himself, if he has had a burning desire to advance in virtue, a love of discipline, a spirit of penance, quick obedience, self-denial and the strength to bear any hardship for the love of Christ. You may do many good things while you are healthy, but when you are sick, I do not know what you may do. Few people are made better by sickness, just as few people are made more holy by visiting churches and shrines.

Do not rely on friends and neighbors, and do not put off your soul's welfare to the future, for people will forget you sooner than you think. It is better to take care of yourself now and to send some good along ahead of you than to trust in the help of others. If you have no care for yourself now, who will care for you in the future? The present time is very precious. Now are the safe days. Now is the acceptable time. But how sad that you do not spend this time well while you have strength to gather the merit which will allow you to live forever! The time will come when you will wish for one day or one hour for changing your ways, and I do not know whether you will get it.

Ah, dear friend! from what great danger can you free yourself and from what great fear can you be freed if you will always be apprehensive and respectful of death. Strive to live in such a way now that in the hour of death you may rejoice rather than fear. Learn now to place Christ at the center of your life, that then you may begin to live your life with Christ. Learn now to let go of all things that stand between you and Christ, that then you may go to Christ freely. Restrain yourself now, that then you may feel confident of your reward.

Ah, my foolish friend! why do you think of living a long life when you are not sure of even one day? How many people are tricked and are unexpectedly snatched away? How often have you heard it said that someone was murdered, someone else drowned, another broke his neck falling from a high place, yet another choked while eating, and someone else met his end while playing; one person died by fire, another from disease, and another was killed by a robber, and thus death is the end of all, and our life passes suddenly like a shadow.

Who will remember you after death, and who will pray for you? Do, do now, dear friend, whatever you can do, because you do not know when you will die, nor do you know what will happen to you afterwards. Gather everlasting riches while you have time. Think of nothing except your eternal well-being. Care only for the things of God. Make friends for yourself now by honoring God's saints and by behaving like them, so that when you pass from this life to the next, they may welcome you home.

Keep yourself as a pilgrim and stranger on earth, a person to whom the affairs of the world mean nothing apart from Christ. Keep your heart free and lifted up to God, for this world is not your permanent home; you are simply passing through. With heartfelt love, direct your prayers and sighs to your eternal home, so that after death your spirit may be worthy to pass happily to the Lord. Amen.

Chapter 24

Of Judgment and Punishment

In everything you do, think of how your life will end and of how you will stand before God. Nothing is hidden from him. He cannot be bribed. He accepts no excuses. He will judge what is right. Oh, my poor friend, what answer will you give to God who knows every bad thing you have ever done—you who sometimes dread the glance of an angry man? Why do you not prepare yourself against the Day of Judgment when no one will be able to excuse or defend another, when each person's burden will be enough for himself alone? Right now your work is fruitful, your tears acceptable, your sighs heard, your sorrow satisfies and cleanses your soul.

A patient person undergoes a great and wholesome cleansing, who, while bearing injuries, grieves more for the evil of others than for his own wrongs; who gladly prays for his enemies, and who truly forgives them; who does not shrink from asking forgiveness from others; who is more easily moved to compassion than to anger; who remains disciplined; and who directs every part of his life to his quest for God. It is better to wash away sins and to nip vices now than to keep them to be purged in the future. Truly, we deceive ourselves by our excessive self-confidence. What else will the fire feed upon but your sins? The more lax you are now and the more you attend to bloating your own self-importance, the more severely will you pay for it later on—and the more fuel will you gather for the burning.

In whatever ways you have sinned, in those same ways will you be severely punished. In hell, the lazy will be spurred with burning goads and the gluttonous tormented with great hunger and thirst. There, the luxurious and the lovers of pleasure will be drenched in burning tar and stinking brimstone, and like mad dogs the envious will howl their anguish. There, no vice will lack its proper torment. There, the proud will be filled with every confusion and the miserly will be in terrible need. There, a single hour of suffering will be worse than a hundred years of the most heavy penance here. There, there is no rest and no comfort for the damned, but here there is sometimes rest from work and we enjoy the solace of our friends.

Be anxious and sorry now about your sins, so that in the Day of Judgment you may be secure among the blessed, for then the righteous will stand firmly against those who have afflicted and oppressed them. Then, the person who humbly submits himself to judgment in this life will become a judge himself. Then, the poor and humble will have great assurance and the proud will quake with fear on all sides. Then, the person who learned to be a fool and to be despised for Christ's sake will be seen to have been wise in this world. Then, all troubles suffered patiently will be pleasing and all injustice will keep quiet. Then, all those who love God will rejoice and all those who do not will mourn. Then, the body that has been afflicted will be exalted more than if it had always been fed on delicious things. Then, poor rags will be splendid and fine clothes will be drab. Then, the poor cottage will be praised more than the gilded palace. Then, steadfast patience will be more useful than all the world's power. Then, simple obedience will stand higher than all worldly cunning. Then, a pure and good conscience will bring more joy than learned philosophy. Then, indifference to riches will weigh more than all the treasures of the world. Then, you will derive more comfort from devout prayer than from fancy food. Then, you will rejoice more in silence than in tedious gossip. Then, holy works will be worth more than eloquent language. Then, an austere life and ardent penance will be more pleasing than all earthly joys.

Teach yourself to endure in small things now, that then you may be freed from heavier pains. Prove here what you can endure hereafter. If you can endure so little now, how will you be able to bear eternal torments? If a little suffering makes you so edgy now, what will hell do then? Surely, you cannot have both kinds of happiness: your every desire in this world and a share in Christ's reign in the next? If, up to this day, you had always lived with honors and pleasures, what good would it all do you if you were to die now? So, all is vanity except to love God and to serve only him, for the person who loves God with his whole heart has no fear of death or judgment or hell, because perfect love gives certain access to God. But to the person who has turned his back on God, it is no wonder if he fears death and judgment! It is good that if love may not recall you from evil, at least the fear of hell may keep you from it. But even so, a person who loses that feeling of deep and abiding love for God will not last long in goodness, but will quickly fall into the snares of the devil.

Chapter 25

Of Improving Our Lives

Be watchful and diligent in God's service, and often think over why you chose to serve Christ in the first place. Was it not that you might live for God and become a spiritual person? Be fervent, then, in going forward, for you will soon receive the reward of your labors, and then there will be no more fear or sorrow in you. By working a little now, you will find great rest later; indeed, you will find endless joy. If you remain faithful and fervent in what you do, God will doubtless be faithful and generous in rewarding you. You must keep good hope of attaining the victory, but you must not become overconfident, lest you grow lazy or self-satisfied.

There was once a certain anxious man who, wavering often between fear and hope and exhausted with grief, prostrated himself in prayer in church before the altar. Turning these things in his mind, he said: "Oh, if only I knew that I shall persevere." On the spot, he heard the divine answer in his own heart: "What if you knew this? What would you do? Do now what you would do then, and you will be very safe.'' Soon after, having been comforted and strengthened, he gave himself up to God's will, and his anxious wavering stopped. He no longer feared for his future; instead, he sought to know God's will for accomplishing today's good works. ''Hope in the Lord and do good,'' says the Prophet, ''and dwell in the land, and you shall be fed with its riches.''

There is one thing that keeps many people from gaining ground and from fervently striving to improve: the dread of difficulty, or more accurately, the effort of the struggle. Those people progress most in virtue—truly, they progress beyond all others—who make a valiant effort to overcome the things that are most troublesome to them, that work most against them. A person makes more progress and deserves fuller grace in those instances where he overcomes such obstacles completely and where he cleanses his spirit by doing so. But not everyone has the same amount to overcome and cleanse. Nevertheless, a person striving diligently to excel will make greater progress—even if he has more to overcome—than will another who is more even-tempered but less keen for virtues.

Two things especially lead to great improvement: the will to drag yourself from the things that will naturally harm you and the desire to pursue the good things that you need the most. You should also watch out for those things that irritate you in other people; when you see them in yourself, get rid of them. Turn everything to your advantage. If you see or hear good examples, imitate them. If you think something is reprehensible, be careful that you do not do the same thing; if you have done it, try to correct yourself quickly. As you watch others, so do they watch you. How joyful and sweet it is to see fervent and devout friends living together agreeably and being well-disciplined. How sad it is—and what a burden!—to see people stumbling along in confusion, not practicing their own vocation. How harmful it is for those same people to neglect the purpose of their calling and to shift their attention to affairs that are none of their concern.

Remember what you set out to do, and place before you the image of the Crucified. When you look into the life of Jesus Christ you may well be ashamed that you have not tried harder to be like him, even though you have followed the ways of God for a long time. A religious person who trains himself intently and devoutly in the holy life and Passion of the Lord will find everything he needs, and he will find it in abundance. He need not look beyond Jesus for anything better. Oh, if the crucified Jesus were to enter into our hearts, how quickly and fully would we be taught!

A fervent, religious person takes all things and bears them well, whatever they may be. A careless and lukewarm person has trouble on top of trouble and endures anguish from every side, because he lacks inner comfort and cannot find it anywhere else. An undisciplined person is open to grave ruin, and a person who looks only for ease and relaxation in life will be limited in his spiritual development, for one thing or another will always displease him.

How do so many other people make do, especially those who are constrained so tightly under monastic vows? They seldom go out, they live apart, they eat the poorest food, they dress coarsely, they work much, they speak little, they watch long, they rise early, they pray long, they read often and they keep control over themselves in every way. Look at the Carthusians, the Cistercians, and the monks and nuns of various religious orders. Every night they rise to sing psalms to the Lord. You should be ashamed of yourself for being so lazy while so many others are praising God even before the sun rises! Oh, if only there were nothing else to do but to praise the Lord our God with all our hearts and voices! Oh, if you never needed to eat or drink or sleep, but could always praise God and could be entirely free to strive after spiritual things; then, you would be much happier than you are now, enslaved as you are by all sorts of necessities. Oh, that there were not such necessities but only the spiritual nourishment of the soul, which, alas, we taste too seldom.

When you come to this, that you look for your comfort from nothing but God, then you begin to know God perfectly; then, too, will you be quite content no matter what happens; then, you will neither rejoice for much nor grieve for little, but will commit yourself wholly and confidently to God, for he means everything to you. To God, nothing passes away or dies, but all things live and all things serve him promptly at a nod.

Always think of the end and that lost time never returns. Without care and diligence you will never acquire virtue. If you begin to grow

apathetic, you will begin to do badly. But if you give yourself enthusias-
tically to your spiritual life, you will find great peace and feel the effort
lighter through God's grace and the love of virtue. The person who
loves God with all his heart and soul—and who faithfully and diligently
acts on that love—is ready for anything. It is greater work to resist our
weaknesses than it is to sweat at manual labor. The person who does not
avoid small faults, little by little slips into greater ones. You will always
be glad at evening if you have spent the day well. Watch over yourself,
rouse yourself, chide yourself, and no matter what others may do, do
not neglect yourself. The more self-disciplined you are, the more you
will progress. Amen.

Here end useful reminders for the spiritual life.

BOOK 2

Suggestions
Drawing One
toward the Inner Life

Chapter 1

Of God Speaking within You

"The kingdom of God is within you," says the Lord. Turn to the Lord with your whole heart, let him be the most important part of your life, and your soul will find rest. If you put God first, you will see his kingdom blossom within you, for the kingdom of God is living in peace and joy with the Holy Spirit, a thing not given to those who do not yearn for him with all their hearts. Christ will come to you and comfort you if you prepare a worthy place for him in your heart. All his glory and beauty lies within you, and he finds great delight in living there. He often visits the person who has a rich inner life, holding sweet conversation with him, granting delightful comfort, much peace and intimate friendship.

So get up, faithful soul, and prepare your heart for this Bridegroom so that he will want to come to you and live in your heart, for he says: "If anyone loves me he will keep my word, and we shall come to him, and we shall make our home with him." Make room for Christ, then, and place him at the center of your life. When he alone rests there, you will have great wealth, and he will be all you need. He will care for you, and he will provide for you faithfully in everything; you will not have to depend on anyone else, for people soon change and they fall short of your expectations before you know it. Only Christ remains constant forever, and he will stand by you to the very end.

Do not rely too heavily on other people, for, like all of us, they have their flaws and foibles. Even if you love someone very much, and that person has been a great blessing to you, do not be disappointed if sometimes the two of you disagree. Those who are your greatest help today may not be tomorrow; their needs change, and so do yours. Place all your trust in God; worship and love him. He will defend you and do what is best for you. This world is not your permanent home; wherever you may be you are a stranger, a pilgrim passing through. You will never find peace unless you are united with Christ in the very depths of your heart.

Why do you look around here to find peace when you do not really belong here? Your place is in heaven, and you should see everything else in terms of heaven. All things pass away, and you pass away with them, too. See that you do not cling to passing things, lest you become caught up in them and perish along with them.

Let your highest thoughts be with the Most High and your prayer be directed to Christ without ceasing. If you cannot contemplate high and heavenly things, rest your thoughts on Christ's Passion, and dwell freely on his Sacred Wounds. If you go for refuge to Jesus's Wounds and to the precious marks of his Passion with humility and love, you will feel great comfort in troubled times, you will not be too concerned about what other people think of you, and it will not be hard to put up with the humiliating things that they may say about you. Christ was also scorned by many people, and in his greatest need he was abandoned by his friends as others heaped insults on his head. Christ was willing to suffer and to be despised, and do you presume to complain of anything? Christ had those who did not like him and those who disagreed with him, and would you have everyone be your friends and supporters? How will your patience be rewarded if you meet with no hardships? If you never encounter opposition, how will you be Christ's friend?

Prop yourself up with Christ and for Christ if you wish to live with Christ. If just once you could perfectly enter the inner life of Jesus and experience a little of his passionate love, then you would not care at all about what you might gain or lose in life. You would even bear insults gladly, for the love of Jesus makes a person think of himself in a very humble way. A lover of Jesus and of truth, a genuinely spiritual person who is free from a troubled heart, can turn himself to God at any time, rise above himself, and rest joyfully in the Lord.

The person who understands all things as they are and not as they are said to be, is truly wise and is taught more by God than by others.

The person who knows how to walk by an inner light is not overly influenced by his surroundings, and he needs neither special places nor special times for prayer. A person who can quickly focus inwardly is at one with himself, because he never completely loses himself in his outside affairs. He is not distracted by such things, nor does occasional necessary business sidetrack him, but he adjusts himself to such things as they come. The person whose inner life is well-ordered and set in place is not troubled by the strange and twisted things that people do. A person is hindered and distracted in life in proportion to the cares he clutters about himself.

If everything were right with you and if you were pure throughout, everything would work to your advantage. As it is, many things often make you unhappy and upset you because you have not successfully shifted your attention from yourself to God, nor have you let go of the things that the world has set in your path. Nothing so stains and entangles a person's heart as a love of material things that is tarnished by self-interest. If you could put aside all those distracting things that the world has to offer, you could then contemplate heavenly things and you would often experience a deep inner joy.

Chapter 2

Of Placing Your Life in God's Hands

Do not be too concerned about who is with you or who is against you, but do be careful that God may be with you in everything you do. Have a good conscience, and God will defend you well, for no one can hurt a person whom God chooses to help. If you know how to be silent and how to put up with your troubles patiently, without a doubt the Lord will help you. He knows when and how to free you, and so you should freely give yourself up to him. It is up to God to help us and to deliver us from all of our problems and uncertainties.

The fact that others know our faults and disapprove of them is often a great help in deepening our humility. When a person humbles himself for his failings he easily satisfies others and he appeases those who are angry with him. God protects and delivers a humble person; he cherishes and consoles him. God gives himself to a humble person; he bestows great grace on him, and after his humiliation he raises him to glory. God reveals his secrets to those who are humble, and he sweetly draws them and calls them to himself. The humble person in the midst of trouble is filled with peace, for he depends on God alone. Do not think that you have made any progress unless you feel truly humble before God and others.

Chapter 3

Of the Good and Peaceful Person

Keep yourself at peace first, and then you will be able to bring peace to others. A person who is at peace with himself does more good than someone who is very learned. A person beset by conflicting passions turns even good things into bad, and he is quick to believe any malicious gossip that comes his way. Someone who is good and peaceful, on the other hand, sees the good side of everything. If you are truly at peace with yourself, you are suspicious of no one, but if you are unhappy and upset, you will be tormented by endless suspicions; you will not be at peace with yourself, nor will you allow others to be at peace. You will often say what you should not, and you will leave undone those things you should do. You will often pry into other people's business and neglect your own. So, first keep careful watch over yourself, and then you may be properly zealous for your neighbor. You are quite adept at excusing and glossing over your own shortcomings, but you are unwilling to accept excuses from anyone else; it would be more just to accuse yourself and to excuse your brother or sister. If you want others to put up with you, you must put up with them.

See how far you still are from true love and humility? A truly loving and humble person does not know how to feel anger or indignation toward others, and if he does, he recognizes such feelings as his own weakness. It is no great thing to associate with good and gentle people, for this naturally pleases all of us; everyone prefers to live in peace, and everyone likes those who think as he does. But to be able to live peacefully with the harsh and wrong-headed or with the unruly or contrary is a great grace and a most praiseworthy and virtuous achievement.

There are some people who are peaceful themselves and who also enjoy peace with others. There are some who neither have peace themselves nor who leave others in peace; they are irksome to others but more irksome to themselves. And there are still others who are peaceful themselves and who try to guide others back to peace. Yet, all the peace we have in this life must be rooted more in humble perseverance than in a lack of difficulties. The person who knows best how to continue on patiently will remain at peace better than anyone else. Such a person is a conqueror of himself and a master of the world, a friend of Christ and heaven's heir.

Chapter 4

Of Pure Feelings and Simple Intentions

Two wings lift a person up from earthly concerns: simplicity and purity. Simplicity should be in intention, purity in feelings. Simplicity reaches out after God, purity catches hold and tastes.

If your heart is free from turmoil and conflict, everything you do will be for the best. If you seek for nothing but the will of God and the good of your neighbor—and if you act accordingly—you will enjoy true freedom. If your heart were right, then everything in God's creation would be a mirror of life and a book of holy teachings. There is no creature so small and worthless that it does not reflect God's goodness. If you were inwardly good and pure, then you would see and understand all things without difficulty. A pure heart penetrates both heaven and hell.

A person's judgment reflects his inner state. If there is joy in the world, surely the person with a pure heart has it, and if there is trouble and anguish anywhere, the person with a bad conscience knows this best. As iron thrust into the fire loses its rust and becomes white-hot, so a person turning wholly to God loses his apathy and is transformed. When a person begins to grow cool, then he shrinks from the smallest effort and willingly accepts comfort from wherever he can get it. But when he begins to master himself and to walk courageously on the path toward God, then those things that earlier weighed him down seem like nothing.

Chapter 5

Of Paying Attention to One's Self

We cannot trust ourselves too much, because we often lack grace and understanding. The light within us is small, and we soon let even this burn out for lack of care. Moreover, we often fail to notice how inwardly blind we are; for example, we frequently do wrong, and to make matters worse, we make excuses about it! Sometimes we are moved by passion and think it zeal. We condemn small things in others and pass over serious things in ourselves. We are quick enough to feel it when others hurt us—and we even harbor those feelings—but we do not notice how much we hurt others. A person who honestly examines his own behavior would never judge other people harshly.

An inward person puts the care of his own soul before all other cares, and a person who attends to himself does not gossip about others. You will never be inward and devout unless you stop talking about other people and start watching over yourself. If you are utterly intent on the state of your own soul and on God, you will not pay so much attention to what other people are doing. When you are not minding your own business, what are you doing? And when you have endlessly meddled in other people's affairs, what will you have gained, having neglected your own soul? If you wish to have peace and true wholeness, you must set aside everything else and tend to your own affairs. You will make great spiritual progress if you keep your nose out of other people's business; you will surely fail if you do not.

Let nothing seem great, high, pleasing or agreeable to you, except God alone and what comes from God. Consider it hollow comfort whatever comes from anything else. The soul that loves God sets little value on anything less than God. God alone, eternal and measureless, fills all. He is the soul's comfort and true joy.

Chapter 6

Of the Joy of a Good Conscience

A good conscience is the best thing a person can have. Have a good conscience, and you will always have joy. A good conscience can bear many things, and it is always joyful in the midst of troubles; a bad conscience is always fearful and uneasy. You may rest easily if your heart does not reproach you. Never be happy unless you have done your best.

Those who do bad things never have true joy nor do they know inner peace, because "there is no peace for the wicked," says the Lord. And if they should say, "We are at peace, nothing bad will happen to us; who will dare to harm us," do not believe them, for God's anger will suddenly rise up, what they do will come to nothing, and all their plans will come crashing down.

To take pride in bearing hardships is not difficult for one who loves Jesus, for to take pride in hardship is to take pride in the Lord's cross. Material success and recognition do not last for long, and, in the end, they always bring sadness with them. If you want to be proud of something, be proud of your good conscience and not of what other people say about you. Your joy should come from God and be in God; your happiness should spring from the truth.

The person who wants true and eternal glory does not care for fleeting glory, and the person who looks for it and thinks highly of it clearly shows that he has little understanding or love for the things of heaven. The person who has great peace of heart pays no attention to either praise or blame. A person whose conscience is clean will easily be content and at peace. Praise does not make you holy; blame does not make you worthless.

What you are, you are. You are no greater than what God sees you to be. If you look after the state of your soul, you will not be bothered by what people say about you. People look at appearances; God looks at the heart. People consider what you have done; God clearly considers your intentions. One sign of a humble soul is that he always does his best and he always considers himself to be unimportant; a sign of great purity and trust is that he does not seek comfort from anyone but God. The person who does not look for praise from other people shows that he has given himself to God completely, "for not he who commends himself is approved," says St. Paul, "but he whom God commends." A spiritual person walks with God in his heart, and he is not won over by what others say and do.

Chapter 7

Of Loving Jesus above All Else

That person is truly blessed who understands what it is to love Jesus and to serve him with deep humility. Jesus wishes to be loved above all things; everything else must come second. The love of anything other than Jesus is deceptive and fickle; the love of Jesus is faithful and enduring. The person who clings to anything other than Jesus falls with its falling; the person who embraces Jesus stands firm forever. Love Jesus and keep him as your friend. When all things fade he will not abandon you, nor will he allow you to perish in the end.

If necessary, you must be willing to let go of everything if Jesus asks it of you. Cling to him in life and in death, and trust yourself to his faithfulness. He alone can help you when all else fails. Your Beloved will not share you with others—that is his nature; he wants to be first in your heart, as you are in his. If you knew how to disentangle yourself from your own confused feelings, Jesus would gladly stay with you.

You will find that whatever hope you have placed in anything other than Jesus is nearly a total loss. Do not trust or lean upon a wind-blown reed, for all flesh is grass, and its glory, like the wild flower's, will fade away. If you trust in appearances, you will quickly be deceived; if you look for comfort and gain in others, you will often be disappointed. If you seek Jesus in everything, you will surely find him, but if you seek yourself, self you will surely find, but to your own ruin. By not seeking Jesus, we hurt ourselves more than the whole world and all our enemies could hurt us.

Chapter 8

Of Intimate Friendship with Jesus

When Jesus is with us, all is right with the world and nothing seems difficult; when he is missing, everything is hard. When Jesus does not speak to the heart, comfort is worthless; but if he speaks only one word, we feel great joy. Did not Mary Magdalen arise at once from where she was weeping when Martha said to her, "the Master is here and is calling for you?" Oh, happy hour when Jesus calls us from tears to spiritual joy!

How dry and hard you are without Jesus! How foolish and empty if you want anything other than Jesus! Is this not a greater loss than if you were to lose the whole world? What can the world offer you without Jesus? To be without Jesus is an unbearable hell, and to be with Jesus is a sweet paradise. If Jesus is with you no foe can harm you. The person who finds Jesus finds a good treasure—indeed, a good beyond all good; the person who loses Jesus loses a very great thing, more than the whole world. It is poverty to live without Jesus; it is wealth to live with him.

To know how to talk with Jesus is a great art, and to know how to cling to him is great wisdom. Be humble and peaceful and Jesus will be with you; be devout and quiet and he will remain with you. You will quickly drive him away and lose his grace, though, if you divert your attention to your own affairs at his expense. And if you drive him away and lose him, to whom will you fly, and who will you then seek as a friend? You cannot live well without a friend, and if Jesus is not your best friend, you will end up being heartbroken and desolate. You act foolishly, then, if you center your life on anything else. It is better to have the whole world against us than to hurt Jesus.

So, from among all those dear to you let Jesus alone be especially loved. Love all things for Jesus's sake, but love Jesus for his own sake. Of all the friends you will find, you should love Jesus Christ in a unique way, for he is the only one who will be good and faithful to the end. Through him and in him love friends and foes alike, and pray that each one may come to know and love him.

Never wish to be more highly praised or more loved than others, for this belongs to God alone who has no equal. Do not wish that anyone should love you and only you, and do not make the same mistake yourself; rather, let Jesus be at the center of all your friendships. Be pure and free of heart, and do not be wrapped up in any other person to the exclusion of Jesus. You should bring a pure, unfettered heart to God if you wish to be free and to see how delightful the Lord is. And truly you will never arrive at this, unless his grace guides you and draws you, so that seeing all things in relation to God, you may be united to him in everything you do.

When the grace of God comes to you, then you are strong in all things, and when it leaves, you become poor and weak, left, as it were, to be beaten and kicked about. You should not be dejected, nor should you despair at this; rather, you should stand with a steady mind toward the will of God and endure whatever comes to you for the praise of Jesus Christ. After winter comes summer, after night the day returns, and after a storm comes great calm.

Chapter 9

Of Emptiness

When we feel at one with God, it is easy not to need others; it is difficult, though, not to need others when God seems to be missing in our lives. To be able to endure feeling rejection and loneliness, to continue on in humility, and not to think that you deserve far better is a real blessing, especially if you can feel this way for the honor of God, and if you do so willingly. Is it such a great thing if you are cheerful and devout when grace is clearly present in your life? Everyone longs for this hour! The person whom God's grace carries has a pleasant enough ride. Is it any wonder if a person feels no burden, being carried by the Almighty and led by the Supreme Guide?

We all gladly cling to some comfort; it is hard not to. The holy martyr, Lawrence, with his great friend and priest, Sixtus, overcame the world because he walked away from everything that the world set between himself and God. Yet, for the love of Christ he patiently bore separation from his dear friend, Sixtus. He overcame his sorrow at losing someone he loved by loving God; he chose to follow God's will instead of his own. Like St. Lawrence, you must also be willing to part with some dear friend if the love of God requires it, and you should not be so deeply hurt when someone you love must leave you. We all know that we must be parted from each other in the end.

We must each wage a long and fierce inner struggle before we learn to master ourselves fully and to focus all of our love on God. When we rely on ourselves, we easily slip into finding comfort in material things and in each other, rather than in God. But one who truly loves Christ—one who pledges himself to a life of holiness—does not fall back on such things, nor does he seek warm, comfortable feelings; he prefers, instead, to endure great tests and hard labor for Christ. So, when God gives you spiritual comfort, receive it gratefully, but know it to be a gift from God, not something you deserve. Do not be puffed up with pride, overly glad, or vainly presumptuous, but be all the more humble because of the gift; also, be hesitant and prudent in all your actions, because this hour will pass, and temptation will surely follow.

When you no longer feel the comfort of God's presence, do not despair right away. With humility and patience, wait for the heavenly visit, for God will return a richer comfort to you than you had before. This is nothing new or strange to those who know God's ways, for the great saints and prophets of old often experienced such changes; whence, the Psalmist, feeling grace present in him, declared, "In my prosperity I said I shall never be moved." But when grace was withdrawn he added what he felt inside, saying: "You hid your face from me, and I became troubled." Yet, in the midst of this, he did not despair but prayed to the Lord all the more earnestly and said: "To you, O Lord, I shall cry and shall beg forgiveness of my God." Finally, his prayer was answered, and he testified that he was heard by saying: "The Lord heard and has had mercy on me: the Lord became my helper." But how? "You have turned my sorrow into joy," he said, "and surrounded me with gladness." If it happened in this way with the great saints, we who are weak and poor should not despair if we are sometimes burning with desire and sometimes not. The Holy Spirit comes and goes according to his good pleasure; whence, blessed Job says: "You visit him at daybreak, and you suddenly test him."

How can I hope then; in whom should I trust, if not in God's great mercy alone and in the sole hope of heavenly grace? For whether I am surrounded by good people, devout brothers and sisters, faithful friends, holy books, or even sweet singing and beautiful hymns, they all offer little help—provide little flavor—when I seem to be abandoned by grace and left in my own poverty. When that happens, there is no better remedy than patience and submission to God's will.

I have never found anyone, however religious and devout, who had not sometimes felt that grace was taken away or who had not felt a lessening of spiritual enthusiasm. All the saints were tempted at one time or another, no matter how caught up and enlightened they were, for a person who is not trained by some trial for God is not worthy of lofty contemplation. Usually, temptation is a sign of comfort to follow, for heavenly comfort is promised to those who are tried by temptations: "He who overcomes," says the Lord, "shall eat of the tree of life."

Divine comfort gives us the strength to bear up under adversity. Temptation then follows, lest we become proud of our goodness. The devil never sleeps, nor is temptation ever far off; therefore, do not cease to prepare yourself for the fight, for there are enemies on both flanks who never rest.

Chapter 10

Of Gratitude for God's Grace

Why do you look for rest when you were born for work? Prepare yourself for enduring hardships rather than for comforts, for bearing the cross rather than for joy. Why, who in this world would not gladly receive spiritual joy and comfort if he could always get it? Spiritual comfort surpasses any delight that you can find in this world, for all worldly delights lack true substance and depth. Only spiritual delights are joyous and honorable, born of virtue and poured into pure souls by God. But no one can enjoy God's comforts whenever he wishes, for temptation is never far off.

A false sense of freedom and excessive self-confidence are great obstacles to such heavenly visits. God does well in granting the grace of spiritual comfort, but we fall short in not referring everything back to God by thanking him. As a result, the gifts of grace cannot flow freely in us because we are often ungrateful to the giver, and we do not refer it all back to the source from which it came. Grace will always be given to the truly grateful, and what is usually given to the humble will be taken away from the proud.

I wish for no divine comfort that blunts the stab of conscience in my heart, nor do I aspire to a lofty contemplation that may lead to spiritual pride. Not everything high is holy nor everything sweet, good nor every desire, pure nor every affection, pleasing to God. I willingly accept that grace which makes me more humble and reverent, more ready to abandon myself into God's hands.

One who has been taught by the gift of grace, and has learned by the pain of its being taken away, will not dare to attribute any good to himself, but will rather admit his poverty and vulnerability. Give to God what is God's, and ascribe to yourself that which is yours; that is, thank God for his grace and claim for yourself alone the guilt for your sins and the punishment they deserve. Always take the lowest place for yourself and the highest will be given to you, for the highest does not exist without the lowest. The saints who are the greatest in God's eyes are the least in their own and the greater their glory, the deeper their humility. Full of truth and heavenly glory, they have no wish for empty praise. Firmly rooted and confident in God, they can in no way be puffed up with themselves. Those who attribute to God all the good that they have received do not seek praise from others, but seek that glory that comes from God alone. Above all, they wish that God may be praised in himself and in all his saints, and this is their constant aim.

So be grateful for every little gift and you will be worthy to receive greater ones. Consider the least gift as great and the most common as something special. If you consider the dignity of the giver, no gift will seem small or unimportant. Nothing given by the most high God is insignificant. And if he should send you pain and sorrow, you ought to be thankful, too, for whatever he permits he does for our own good. The person who wishes to keep God's grace should be thankful when it is given, and he should be patient when it is taken away. Pray for its return, then be cautious and humble lest it be lost.

Chapter 11

O f the Few Who Love Jesus's Cross

Jesus has many lovers of his heavenly kingdom these days, but few of them carry his cross. He has many who desire comfort, but few who desire affliction. He has many friends to share his meals, but few to share his fasts. Everyone is eager to rejoice with him, but few are willing to endure anything for him. Many follow Jesus up to the breaking of the bread, but few as far as drinking from the chalice of his Passion. Many admire his miracles, but few pursue the shame of the cross. Many love Jesus as long as no difficulties touch them. Many praise and bless him as long as they receive comfort from him. But if Jesus hides himself and leaves them awhile, they either complain or fall into a deep depression.

Those who love Jesus for himself and not for their own comfort bless him in every trial and heartfelt anguish, just as they do in moments of great comfort. And even if he should never give them comfort, they would still always praise him and always want to thank him. Oh, how powerful is a pure love of Jesus, untainted by self-interest or self-love! Can we not call all those people mercenaries who are constantly seeking spiritual comfort? Do they, who are forever thinking of their own comfort and gain, not prove that they love themselves more than they love Christ? Where shall we find a person who is willing to serve God without receiving something in return?

Seldom do we find a person so spiritual that he lives stripped of everything. Who can find someone truly poor in spirit and totally detached from all the things of this world? His price is well beyond that of anything on earth! If a person were to give up all his possessions, that would still be nothing. And if he were to do great penance, it would still be a little thing. And if he were to learn all knowledge, he would still be far off. And if he had great virtue and burned with a passionate devotion, still much would be lacking in him; that is, the one thing which is supremely necessary. And what is it? That having left all things behind, he must also leave himself—totally abandon himself—keeping nothing of his selfish, self-centered ways. And when he has done all that he knows must be done, then let him believe that he has done nothing. Let him not be deluded when others praise him, but let him admit in all honesty that he is only a humble servant of God. As Truth himself has said: "When you have done all that is asked of you, say to yourselves, we are unworthy servants." Then he will be truly poor and naked in spirit, and he may say with the Prophet: "I am alone and poor." Yet, no one is richer, no one more powerful, no one more free than the person who can give his whole life to God and freely serve others with deep humility and love.

Chapter 12

Of the Royal Road of the Holy Cross

To many people this saying seems harsh: "Deny yourself, take up your cross and follow Jesus." But it will be much harsher to hear that final word: "Depart from me, you accursed, into everlasting fire." They who gladly hear and follow the word of the cross now will have nothing to fear later on when they hear of eternal damnation. This sign of the cross will be in the heavens when the Lord comes to judge. Then all the servants of the cross who, in life, conformed themselves to the Crucified Lord, will approach Christ the Judge with great confidence.

Why then are you afraid to take up the cross, the way that leads to the kingdom of God? In the cross is salvation; in the cross is life; in the cross is protection; in the cross is heavenly sweetness; in the cross is strength of mind; in the cross is spiritual joy; in the cross is supreme virtue; in the cross is perfect holiness. There is no salvation for the soul nor hope for eternal life, except in the cross.

So take up your cross and follow Jesus, and you will go on to eternal life. He went before you carrying his cross, and on the cross he died for you, that you too may carry your cross, and that you too may die on the cross. If you die with him, you will live with him. If you join him in suffering, you will join him in glory. Listen closely. Everything is founded on the cross, and everything consists in dying on it, and there is no other road to life and to true inner peace than the road of the holy cross and of our daily dying to ourselves. Walk where you will, seek where you will, and you will find no loftier way above nor safer way below than the way of the holy cross.

Plan as you like and arrange everything as best you can, yet you will always encounter some suffering whether you want to or not. Go wherever you will, you will always find the cross. Either you will feel physical pain or spiritual pain. Sometimes God will leave you, and sometimes a neighbor will upset you; even worse, you will sometimes be a burden to yourself! You can find neither remedy nor comfort which can free you or relieve you, but you must bear it as long as God wishes. God wants you to learn to endure troubles without comfort, to submit yourself totally to him, and to become more humble through adversity.

No one feels in his heart what Christ felt in his Passion, except the person who suffers as he did. So, the cross is always ready and waits for you everywhere. You cannot escape it no matter where you run, for wherever you go you are burdened with yourself, and wherever you go, there you are. Look up, look down; look out, look in. Everywhere you will find the cross, and you must endure patiently if you wish to have inner peace and gain eternal life.

If you bear your cross willingly, it will carry you and lead you to your desired goal where suffering will end, but that cannot happen here. If you bear your cross unwillingly, you will make a greater burden for yourself—and you must still carry it, in any case. If you fling aside one cross, you will certainly find another and, perhaps, a heavier one.

Do you expect to escape what no one has ever avoided? What saint was there in the world without crosses and afflictions? Not even our Lord Jesus Christ spent one hour without the anguish of his Passion as long as he lived. It was necessary that Christ should suffer and rise again from the dead and so enter into his glory. So why do you seek another way, different from the royal road, which is the way of the holy cross?

Christ's entire life was a cross and a martyrdom, and will you look for rest and happiness? You are deluded if you look for anything other than affliction, for our entire mortal life is surrounded by crosses. And the more we progress in the spiritual life, the heavier our crosses will be, for the pain of our separation from God increases in proportion to our love of God.

But one who bears many crosses is not without some comfort, for he knows the great rewards that will come to him by patiently accepting God's will. At the same time that he bends under the weight of his cross, his burden is changed into divine comfort, for he knows that God will reward him for his efforts. And the more a person's body is weakened by affliction, the more his spirit is strengthened by inner grace. Sometimes, through the love of conforming himself to Christ's cross, a person is so comforted by his trials and afflictions that he does not want to be without them, for he believes that the more and heavier burdens he can bear for Christ, the more acceptable he will become to him. For such a person, patiently living out God's will becomes a blessing.

It is not our strength but Christ's grace which can and does accomplish such great things in us. Christ's grace enables us to embrace warmly those things from which we naturally recoil. It is not in our nature to bear the cross, to love the cross, to discipline ourselves, to avoid seeking praise, to suffer insults willingly, to think humbly of ourselves, to appear humble to others, to endure adversity and loss, and not to seek prosperity as our first goal. If you take a look at yourself, you will see that you can do none of this alone, but if you confide in the Lord, he will give you heavenly strength and all that you have chosen to do will become easier. You will not even fear your enemy, the devil, if you are armed with faith and sealed with the cross of Christ.

So, as a good and faithful servant of Christ, brace yourself to bear the Lord's cross with valor; out of love for you he was nailed to it. Be ready to bear many hardships and every kind of misfortune, for you will surely experience them wherever you are and wherever you may try to hide. It must be so. There is no way to avoid it; you can only endure it patiently. Drink lovingly of the chalice of the Lord if you wish to be his friend and to share his life. Leave all divine comforts to God; let him deal with them as he chooses. As for you, be ready to bear up under afflictions and consider them to be great consolations. For even if you were to endure all the world's suffering all by yourself, it would still be nothing compared to the future glory that only a little suffering would earn for you.

When you have come to this, that enduring pain and sorrow for Christ's sake is sweet and pleasing to you, then think that all is well with you, for you have found paradise on earth. As long as suffering is hard for you and you seek to avoid it, all will go wrong with you, and the very trouble that you run from will hound you wherever you go. If you resign yourself to what must be—that is, that we must all suffer and die—you will feel much better, and you will find peace. Even if you were caught up to the third heaven with St. Paul, that would be no guarantee that you will not suffer adversity. "I shall show him," said Jesus, "how much he must suffer for my name." So, it remains for you to suffer if you wish to love Jesus and to serve him always.

If only you were worthy of enduring something for the name of Jesus! What great glory would be yours! How much joy would you give to God's saints! What an example you would be to your neighbor! For everyone praises a willingness to endure hardships, but only a few are willing to do it. So, you gladly ought to suffer a little for Christ; many people suffer much heavier things for the world.

Know for certain that you must lead a life that focuses less and less on yourself. The less self-centered you become, the more you become centered in God. You are not fit to understand heavenly things unless you resign yourself to bearing adversities for Christ. Nothing is more pleasing to God, and nothing is better for you in this world than to be willing to suffer for Christ. If you had the choice, you would choose to suffer adversities for Christ rather than to be comforted and put at ease, for you would be more like Christ, more like all the saints. Our worth and our spiritual progress do not rest on warm feelings and God-given comforts, but rather on patiently enduring great calamities and trials.

If there had been anything better, anything more suited or more useful to our salvation than suffering, Christ surely would have pointed it out to us by his word and example. For the disciples who followed him and for all those who wish to follow him, he clearly urges carrying the cross, saying: "If anyone would come after me, let him deny himself and take up his cross and follow me." So, let all your reading and studying end on this note: To enter the kingdom of God, we must endure many hardships.

Here End Suggestions Drawing One toward the Inner Life.

BOOK 3

Of
Inner Comfort

f Christ Speaking in Your Own Heart

Disciple:

I shall listen to what the Lord God will say deep within my heart. Blessed is the soul that listens to the Lord speaking within and that receives a word of comfort from him. Blessed are the ears that are attuned to the soft whisper of God's voice and that ignore the buzzing of the world. Blessed indeed are the ears that pay no attention to outside clamor, but listen to truth teaching from within. Blessed are the eyes that are closed to outside things, but are intent on inner things. Blessed are they who plumb their own depths and by daily efforts prepare themselves to understand the secrets of heaven. Blessed are they who are completely free to attend to God and who have shaken off everything that stands in their way. Mark these things, my soul; be silent, and visit the quiet recesses of your own heart. It is there that you will hear God's voice.

Jesus:

I am your salvation, your peace and your life; live in me, and you will find peace. Let go of all passing things, and seek eternal ones. What are all passing things but enticements that lead you away from me? And what good are created things, if they cause you to be abandoned by the Creator? So, let go of all such things and make yourself pleasing and faithful to your Creator, so that you may find true happiness.

Chapter 2

hat Truth Speaks Quietly to the Heart

Disciple:

Speak, Lord, for your servant is listening. I am your servant; give me understanding that I may know your ways. Incline my heart to your words, and let your speech come upon me as dew upon the grass. In days gone by the children of Israel said to Moses, "Speak to us and we shall listen; do not let the Lord speak to us, lest we die." This is not how I pray, Lord. No. With the great prophet Samuel, I humbly and earnestly beg: "Speak, Lord, for your servant is listening."

Do not let Moses or any other prophet speak to me. You speak to me, O Lord God, you who inspire and enlighten all the prophets, for you alone, without them, can perfectly instruct me, while they without you can do nothing. They indeed can utter words, but they cannot convey the spirit of those words. They say beautiful things, but with you silent, they do not set the heart on fire. They convey the letter, but you reveal the meaning. They pronounce the mysteries, but you unfold their secrets. They declare the commandments, but you help us to practice them. They point out the way, but you give us the strength to walk it. They work only from the outside, but you instruct and enlighten the heart. They water the surface, but you provide a rich harvest. They proclaim the words, but you give understanding to what we hear.

So, do not let Moses speak to me, but you, O Lord, my God, eternal Truth, you speak to me. If I hear your voice, I may not die dry and barren as I would if I were warned from without and not inflamed from within. If I hear your voice, may I not be condemned for hearing the word and not following it, for knowing it and not loving it, for believing it and not living it. Speak then, Lord, for your servant listens, for you have the words of eternal life. Speak to me to comfort my soul and to change my whole life; in turn, may it give you praise and glory and honor, forever and ever.

Chapter 3

hat We Should Listen to God's Words with Deep Humility and Serious Intent

Jesus:

My dear friend, listen to my words, words of sweetness that surpass those of all the philosophers and wise people of this world. My words are spirit and life and are not to be measured by human understanding. They are not to be brought out to pass idle moments, but they are to be heard in silence and taken up with deep humility and profound love.

Disciple:

Blessed is that person whom you instruct, O Lord, whom you teach in your own way. By your teaching, you give him rest from difficult days that he may know you are with him.

Jesus:

I taught the prophets from the beginning and even now I have not ceased to speak, but many people cannot hear my voice, for they have chosen not to listen. They are more eager to hear what the world has to say than to listen to God, and they are more hungry for what the world has to offer than for what pleases God.

The world promises trivial things that last but a moment, and it is served with rapacious greed; I promise the sum of all eternal things, and many people's hearts remain indifferent. How many serve and obey me in all things with the same care and attention that they give to the world and its masters? They should be ashamed of themselves. And why? Listen. For a small gain people will run a long way, but for eternal life many will scarcely lift a foot from the ground. They want to be paid for their every effort, and sometimes they quarrel shamefully over pocket change; they are not afraid to exhaust themselves working day and night for a small profit or for the promise of a promotion mentioned in passing. But alas! for a permanent good, for a priceless gain, for the highest honor and a never-ending glory, they shrink from the least sign of an effort.

They should be ashamed, then, those lazy and grumbling people who are more ready to lose their souls than they are to gain life. They are more joyful over an empty illusion than they are over the truth. Sometimes their hopes come to nothing, but my promise misleads no one, nor does it send away empty-handed anyone who trusts in me. What I have promised, I shall give; what I have said, I shall do, so long as a person remains faithful in loving me until the end. I am the one who rewards all good people and the one who says "yes" to all those who follow me. Write my words on your heart and earnestly reflect upon them, for you will need them in times of trial.

What you do not understand through your reading and studying, you will know when I come to you. I usually visit those I love in two ways: I mean, of course, in temptation and in comfort. And every day I offer them two lessons: one pointing out their faults and the other encouraging them to grow in virtue. The person who rejects me and does not accept my words does so with the full knowledge that on the last day it is I who will be his judge.

Disciple:

A Prayer Asking for the Grace of Devotion

O Lord, my God, you are all the good I have. And who am I that I dare speak to you? I am the poorest of your servants, a commonplace creature, much more poor and insignificant than I know or dare to say. Remember, Lord, that I am nothing; I have nothing; I am worth nothing, without you. You alone are good, just and holy; you can do all things; you give all things; you fill all things. Only that person who chooses to turn his back on you, do you leave empty and alone.

Remember your mercies, and fill my heart with your grace, you who do not want your works to be for nothing. How can I live with myself in this unhappy life unless your mercy and grace comfort me? Do not turn your face from me, do not delay coming to me, do not take away the comfort of your love, lest my soul be like a parched land, thirsty for you.

O Lord, teach me to do your will; teach me to stand in your presence in a worthy and humble way, for you are my Wisdom, you who truly know me, who knew me before the world began and before I was born into it.

Chapter 4

hat We Should Live in God's Presence in Truth and Humility

Jesus:

My dear friend, walk before me in truth, and always look for me in the simplicity of your own heart. The person who walks with me as his companion will be protected from all evil, and the truth will free him from from all deceit. If the truth sets you free, you will be truly free, and you will be unconcerned about what others may have to say.

Disciple:

Lord, it is true. Let it be done to me as you say. May your truth teach me, guard me and keep me until I arrive at my salvation. Let your truth free me from every wrong feeling and every confused thought, and I shall walk with you in great freedom of heart.

Jesus:

I shall teach you what is right and pleasing to me. With deep sorrow and regret, think of all the times you have failed me, and never congratulate yourself because you have done something good. The fact is you are a sinner, subject to and trapped by many conflicting passions. Left to yourself you always move toward nothingness; you easily fall to ruin; you are easily overcome, easily upset, easily weakened. Of yourself, you have nothing to be proud of, but many things ought to humble you, for you are weaker than you know. So, let nothing you do seem great to you. Let nothing seem grand, nothing priceless and admirable, nothing worthy of great praise, nothing high, nothing truly desirable, except that which is eternal.

Let the eternal truth please you above all things, and let your own sinfulness always displease you. Fear nothing, abhor and run from nothing, as much as from your own sins; they should displease you more than the loss of any possession you may have.

Some people do not walk with me honestly, but led by curiosity and arrogance, they want to know my inner thoughts and understand the sublime mysteries of God, heedless of themselves and their salvation. I see their pride and curiosity for what they are, and such people often fall into great temptations and sins because of them. Fear God's judgments. Dread the Almighty's anger. Do not presume to probe the works of the Most High, but look into your own failings, into how far you have fallen short, and into how many good things you have neglected to do.

Some people carry their devotion with them only in books, others in holy pictures, and others in outward signs and symbols. Some have me on their lips, but little in their hearts. There are others who, having an enlightened mind and pure feelings, always yearn for eternal things, listen with a weary heart to the latest news and gossip, and deal with the world's problems, and their own, as best they can. Such people understand what the Spirit of Truth speaks within them, for it teaches them to subordinate earthly things to heavenly ones; to see beyond the concerns of the moment, and to long for heaven day and night.

Chapter 5

f the Wonderful Effects of God's Love

Disciple:

I bless you, Father in heaven, Father of my Lord, Jesus Christ, for you have seen fit to remember me in my poverty. O Father of mercies and God of all consolation, I thank you for sometimes renewing my life with your consolations, I who am so unworthy of them. I ever bless and glorify you, together with your only-begotten Son and the Holy Spirit, the Comforter, forever and ever.

O Lord God, my holy lover, when you enter my heart everything rejoices within me. You are my glory and the joy of my heart. You are my hope and my refuge in the day of my distress. But because I am still frail in love and flawed in virtue, I need to be comforted and consoled by you. Come to me often and teach me the ways of holiness. Free me from all evil, and heal my heart of all confusion. Once I am healed and cleansed within, I may then be able to love you as I should; I may then be strong in suffering and steadfast in pressing on.

Love is a great thing, a great good in every way, for it alone lightens every burden and passes smoothly over all misfortunes. Love carries a burden without feeling it and makes every bitter thing sweet and savory. The noble love of Jesus spurs us on to do great things and excites us always to long for perfection. Love wants to soar to the heights and not be tied down by anything low. Love wants to be free, unencumbered and whole, lest its inner vision be clouded by any momentary gain or temporary setback.

Nothing is sweeter than love, nothing stronger, nothing more sublime, nothing more expansive, nothing more joyful, nothing more abundant or better in heaven or on earth. Love is born of God; in the end, it rests in nothing other than God. A person who loves may soar, run and rejoice; he is free and nothing holds him back. He gives all for all and has all in all, since above all he rests in that one highest good, from whom all good springs and flows. He does not look at the gifts he receives, but he turns himself beyond all gifts to the giver.

Love often knows no limit, but exceeds all limits. Love feels no burden, shrugs off all labor, aims beyond its strength, and refuses to admit impossibility. Because love believes that it can accomplish anything, it does.

Love keeps watch, and sleeping keeps one eye open. Tired, it is not wearied; constrained, it is not bound; frightened, it is not terrified, but like a living flame or burning torch it mounts upward, passing through unharmed. Whoever loves recognizes this voice: "My God! my Love! You are all mine and I am all yours!" It is the cry of an ardent soul deeply in love with God.

Stretch wide my love so that I may learn to taste how sweet it is to love, to dissolve in love, to swim in it. Let me be gripped by love, soaring beyond myself through boundless passion and wonder. Let me sing love's song. Let me follow you, my beloved, on high. Let my soul, exalting in love, lose itself in your praise. Let me love you more than myself, and let me love myself only for love of you. Let me love you in all others who truly love you, as the law of love, which shines from you, commands.

Love is swift, honest, devout, joyous and pleasing; love is strong, patient, faithful, prudent, long-suffering, courageous. Love is never self-seeking, for when we seek ourselves, we abandon love. Love is watchful, humble and upright; it is not soft, not frivolous, not given to empty things; it is sober, chaste, steadfast, calm, and it always stays alert. Love is submissive and obedient; it is ordinary and insignificant in its own eyes, devout and grateful to God, always trusting and hoping in him, even when it cannot taste him, for one does not know love without pain.

The person who is not ready to suffer all things and to do all things that his beloved asks, does not deserve to be called a lover. For the sake of the beloved, a lover should willingly embrace every hardship and bitterness and not turn away from his beloved when things go wrong.

Chapter 6

f the Proof of a True Lover

Jesus:

My dear friend, you are not yet a courageous and wise lover.

Disciple:

Why, Lord?

Jesus:

Because at the least little hardship you drop what you are doing and you impatiently look around for a word of comfort from anyone who happens to be close at hand. A courageous lover remains firm in the midst of temptation and does not cave in to the cunning suggestions of the enemy. As I please you in good times, so I shall not displease you in bad times.

The wise lover does not consider so much the lover's gift, as the giver's love. He pays more attention to the giver's affection than to the gift's value, and he places less value on all gifts than he does on the be-loved. The noble lover is not satisfied with the gift, but he desires me above all gifts. So all is not lost if you sometimes feel less affectionate toward me and my saints than you would like. That good and sweet feel-ing which you sometimes experience is the result of grace being present, a little sample of your heavenly home. Do not depend on it too much, for it comes and goes.

To fight against all evil thoughts that come to mind and to scorn the devil's urgings are signs of great virtue and merit. So do not let strange fantasies trouble you, no matter what kind they may be. Keep your reso-lutions firmly, and be faithful to God. Sometimes you may be suddenly seized by intense spiritual feelings and seem to soar toward heaven, and then, just as quickly, you may seem to drop back to earth, back to your own foolish thoughts. Such feelings are not illusions. Enjoy them when you feel them, and be thankful for them, but do not seek them out. Chas-ing after such feelings can consume you. Try, instead, to maintain a spiritual calm; in the end, it will help you more.

Know that the old enemy strives in every way he can to block your doing good and to keep you from your religious devotions: from honor-ing the saints, from devoutly remembering my Passion, from usefully recalling your sins, from keeping watch over your heart, and from firmly resolving to advance in virtue. He whispers evil thoughts into your ears, so that he may wear you out and frighten you, and so that he may pull you from prayer and reading. Humble confession offends him, and if he could, he would prevent you from receiving Holy Commu-nion. Do not believe him or pay attention to him, even though he has often set his traps to ensnare you. Throw it right back at him when he suggests foul and wicked things to you! Say to him: "Get out of here, foul spirit; shame on you, miserable wretch! You are filthy to utter such things in my ears! Get away from me you disgusting creature! You shall have no part of me, but Jesus will be with me as a courageous warrior, and you will stand confounded! I would rather die and endure any pain than give in to you! Be quiet and keep still! I shall hear no more of you, though you continue to molest me! The Lord is my light and my salva-tion; whom shall I fear? Though an entire army may encamp against me, my heart shall not be afraid! The Lord is my helper and my redeemer!''

Fight bravely, and if you sometimes fall through weakness, rise up again with greater strength than before, sure of my greater grace. Take care, too, to guard against self-satisfaction and pride. By these many people are drawn astray, and they sometimes fall into an almost incurable blindness. Many people have met their ruin through pride and self-reliance. Let it be a warning to you and a continuous source of humility.

Chapter 7

f **Protecting Grace with Humility**

Jesus:

My friend, it is more to your advantage—and it is safer, too—to keep your private devotions to yourself. The way you worship God on your own is a great grace; do not flaunt it or talk much about it or think much about it. Instead, keep it to yourself, and be wary of it as a thing given to someone who does not deserve it. Never cling too tightly to these holy feelings, for they can quickly change to the opposite.

When you enjoy such grace, think how poor and ineffectual you are without it. Progress in the spiritual life comes not so much when you experience comforting grace, as when, with humility and resignation, you live patiently with its being taken away. When it is, you should not grow lazy in your prayers nor should you allow your other duties to slide. Instead, cheerfully do the best you can, and do not give up on yourself entirely because your soul feels dry or your mind worried.

Yes, there are many who quickly become impatient or lazy when things do not go well with them. A person does not always choose his own path, and it is for God to give comfort when he wants, as much as he wants, and to whom he wants.

Some unwary people have brought themselves to ruin through their private devotions, for they wished to do more than they could. They did not consider how frail they really are; they followed their hearts instead of their reason. And because they presumed to do more than please God, they soon lost his grace. They tried building a nest for themselves in heaven; instead, they became poor and abject. Then, humiliated and poverty stricken, they realized at last that if they wanted to fly, they had to depend on my wings, not their own.

Those who are new and inexperienced in the ways of the Lord can easily be disappointed and broken unless they keep watch over themselves, as wise people advise. But if they choose to follow their own feelings rather than the experience of others, they will jeopardize reaching their goal—that is, as long as they are unwilling to set aside their presumption. People who think themselves wise are seldom humble enough to allow others to guide them. It is better to be stupid and slow and to be humble about it, than to possess vast knowledge and to be smug about it. It is better for you to have a little than a lot, if a lot only makes you proud.

The person who takes spiritual joy for granted, oblivious of his former poverty and the chaste fear of losing what little grace he has, lacks discretion. Neither does a person show enough courage, who caves in to despair at the time of adversity, thinking thoughts and harboring feelings that show less trust in me than he should.

A person who wishes to be too secure in time of peace will often be depressed and afraid in time of war. If you knew how to stay always humble and small in your own eyes and how to tame and direct your spirit, you would not so easily fall into danger and encounter road blocks. This is good advice: When the spirit begins to grow warm, think what the future may be like with the light of my fire gone. And when this happens, remember that the light which I withdrew for a time, as a warning to you and for my glory, may return again.

Such a trial is often more helpful for you than if you always had things go your way, for a person's worth is not measured by whether he has many visions or spiritual comforts, whether he is deeply read in scripture, or whether he holds a high position. A person is highly valued by God, if he is grounded in true humility and filled with love, if he always seeks God's honor with purity and integrity, if he has a humble opinion of himself, if he sincerely dislikes his selfish nature, and even if he does not mind being looked down upon and belittled by others, instead of being honored.

Chapter 8

f Humility before God

Disciple:

I shall speak to my Lord, though I may be dust and ashes. If I think myself better than I am, then you, Lord, show me that I am not. My sins speak out the lie, and I can say nothing to the contrary. But if I humble myself, think of myself as nothing, sweep away all self-importance, and account myself as dust, as indeed I am, then your grace will be mine. Then your light will be close to my heart, and all self-importance, no matter how little, will remain submerged in the valley of my nothingness and will perish forever. There, in my nothingness, you show me to myself—what I am, what I have been, and what I have become. I am nothing, and I did not even know it.

If left to myself, I am nothing; I am all weakness. But if you turn your face upon me, I am at once made strong and am filled with new happiness. It is wonderful that I am so quickly uplifted and so kindly embraced by you, I who by my own weight am always sinking to the bottom. Your love does this. It freely goes before me and helps me in my many needs. It guards me from grave dangers, too. To tell the truth, your love protects me from so many evils that I cannot count them all!

By seeking myself, I lost myself; by seeking you alone, and by loving you with a pure love, I found both myself and you. And through this love I have more profoundly returned to my nothingness, for you, O sweet Lord, you treat me far better than I deserve, beyond all that I dare to hope or to ask for.

May you be blessed, my God, for though I am unworthy of all the good things you give me, yet your excellence and infinite goodness never cease giving them. Even the thankless and those who have turned their backs on you receive your blessing. Turn us back to you, so that we may be thankful, humble, and devout, for you are our salvation, our courage, and our strength.

Chapter 9

hat All Things Come from God and Must Return to God

Jesus:

My friend, I must be your supreme and final end if you wish to be truly blessed. If I am, your love will be purified and not be twisted back on yourself and on the things of this world, as it so often is. If you seek yourself in anything, you quickly weaken and dry up inside. Therefore, refer all things to me as to the beginning, for everything you have has come from me. Look upon it all as flowing from the highest good; that being the case, all things must return to me as to their source.

All people, small and great, rich and poor, draw living water from me as from a quick-springing well, and they who serve me freely and of their own accord shall receive grace upon grace. But the person who seeks fulfillment in anything but me, or who seeks happiness in some private good of his own making, will not find true joy nor a heart overflowing with love; instead, he will encounter a mountain of obstacles and anxieties. Therefore, you should not take credit for any good qualities that you might have nor should you attribute any special depth of character to anyone else; instead, give God credit for everything, for without him we have nothing.

I have given you everything and I wish it all to come back to me, and I would like for you to thank me for the gifts that I have given you; this is a truth that makes pride vanish. If heavenly grace and true love become part of you, there will be no more envy or rancor or self-love, for divine love conquers everything and opens out the powers of your soul to encompass the whole world.

If you are truly wise, you will find joy in me alone and hope in me alone, for no one is good but God alone. Praise him and bless him in everything you do.

Chapter 10

f How Good It Is to Serve God

Disciple:

Now I shall speak again, Lord, and I shall not be silent. I shall say to my God, my Lord and my King, who is on high: "Oh, how great is the abundance of your sweetness, Lord, which you have in store for those who love you." But what are you to those who love you? What for those who serve you with all their heart? Contemplating you is a sweetness beyond words. Oh, how much you lavish on those who love you!

You have shown me the sweetness of your love in these ways: that when I had no being you made me; that when I strayed far from you, you brought me back again to serve you, and you taught me how to love you. O font of eternal love, what may I say of you? How can I ever forget you, you who have seen fit to remember me, even when I wasted away and became lost? You have shown mercy to your servant beyond all hope, and you have granted grace and friendship beyond all deserving.

What am I to give you in return for such grace? For it is not given to everyone to give up everything, to set aside the world, and to take up the monastic life. Is it a great thing to serve you, whom all creation is bound to serve? It should not seem so special for me to serve you. Rather, this should seem great and marvelous to me: that you stoop to accept in service one so poor and unworthy and count him among your beloved friends.

Hear me, Lord! All that I have is yours, and all the gifts that I use to serve you belong to you. Yet, you serve me more than I serve you. Imagine! heaven and earth, which you created for our use, stand before you, and each day they carry out your every command! And this is only a small thing. Why, you have appointed even the angels to serve mankind! But even more astounding is that you yourself have stooped to serve us and have promised that you will give yourself to us!

What shall I give you in return for these countless blessings? If only I could serve you all the days of my life! If only I were able to serve you worthily, even for one day! Truly, you are worthy of all service, all honor and eternal praise. You are my Lord, and I am your poor servant, who is bound to serve you with all my strength and without ever growing tired of praising you. This is what I want; this is what I desire, and whatever is lacking in me, please add it.

It is a great honor, a great glory, to serve you and to hold all other things as unimportant when compared to you. Those people will have much grace, who willingly submit themselves to your most holy service. They will experience the sweet comfort of the Holy Spirit, who, because of their love of you, have cast aside all worldly ambition. They will gain great freedom of mind, who, for your name, enter on the narrow path and wish only to journey to you. O delightful and joyous service of God, by which we are made truly free and holy! O holy state of religious service, which makes us equal to angels, pleasing to God, terrible to devils, and commendable to all the faithful! O cherished and ever-desired service that wins the highest good and attains a joy that lasts forever!

Chapter 11

hat Feelings May Not Always Be What They Seem

Jesus:

My dear friend, you still have many things to learn which you have not yet fully grasped.

Disciple:

What are these things, Lord?

Jesus:

You should make my will your own, stop being enamored of yourself, and eagerly do what I ask of you. Enthusiasm often drives you to action, but take the time to learn whether what you do is for me or for yourself. If I am the reason, you will be quite satisfied with whatever I shall decide for you; if your motive is selfish, though, it will get in your way and burden your conscience. Take care, then, not to rely too much on what you want without consulting me. You may find that what at first seems like the right thing to do, in the end will leave you upset and sorry. Do not be so quick to follow every good feeling, nor so eager to avoid every bad one.

It is sometimes wise to hold yourself in check, even when you are doing good things. An all-encompassing passion can sap your energy, offend other people, and lead to discouragement when others do not share your interest. Sometimes you must use extreme measures to resist your enthusiasms, for you will be torn in two directions. In every case, though, talk with me, then follow the voice of your conscience. It will not lead you astray. Be content with little; be happy with what is simple; and do not grumble if things seem to take a different turn from what you expected.

Chapter 12

f Patience

Disciple:

Lord God, as I see it, patience is very necessary for me, because many troubles befall us in this life. No matter what I do to live in peace, my life cannot be without struggle and sorrow.

Jesus:

So it is, dear friend. But I do not want you to look for an easy peace. Think instead that you have found true peace when it has been well-tested by trouble and hardship. If you say that you cannot bear such suffering, how will you endure the flames of purgatory? Always choose the lesser of two evils; to avoid eternal punishment in the future, do all that you can to bear present troubles patiently.

Do you think that worldly people suffer nothing, or perhaps only suffer a little? You will not find it so, even if you search among the most wealthy and self-indulgent. But, you will say, they have many luxuries and they do what they please, so they make light of their troubles. Granted, they have whatever they want, but how long do you think it will last? Look, the rich of this world will vanish like smoke; in the end, no one will even remember them. Even now they do not enjoy their riches without bitterness, weariness and fear. The very things that bring them delight also bring them pain and sorrow. And rightly so. Because they live for passing pleasures, they cannot find lasting fulfillment. Confusion and bitterness touch all they do.

Oh, how brief, how false, how excessive, and how ugly is such a way of life. People do not know how drunk and blind they are! Like dumb beasts, for a trifling pleasure in this life, they rush headlong into spiritual death. Do not chase after such things, my dear friend. Turn away from your self-centered desires, find joy in me, and I will give you what your heart truly desires. In fact, if you wish to know real delight and comfort, walk away from anything that stands between you and me. The more often you place me at the center of your life, the more often will you feel great comfort and sweetness.

But at first you will feel sorrow and conflict. A deep-rooted habit will resist, but it will be overcome by a better habit. You may grumble, but spiritual warmth will win you over. The old serpent will tempt you and entice you, but he will be sent packing by prayer, and if you do some useful work in the meantime, you will block his chief approach.

Chapter 13

f Obedience and Humility

Jesus:

My dear friend, if a person living under monastic vows shrinks from obedience, he also shrinks from God's grace. Likewise, if a person living the monastic life seeks only what is best for himself, he does so at the expense of the common good. If such a person does not freely and willingly submit himself to his superior, it is a sign that he has not come very far in his vocation. So, learn to obey your superior promptly if you wish to progress. The old enemy is more quickly overcome if your own heart is not in shambles.

When you are not in perfect harmony with yourself, you are your own worst enemy. You must do away with every trace of self-centeredness, if you wish to overcome your weaknesses. It is your stubborn self-will that stands in the way of your obedience. Why is it so remarkable if you, who are dust and nothingness, submit yourself to another person for God's sake, when I, the Almighty and Most High, who created all things out of nothing, humbly subjected myself to others for you? I became the most humble and abject of all, so that you might conquer your pride through my humility.

So, learn to obey, dust. Learn to humble yourself, earth and clay, and to think of others before you think of yourself. Learn to live in obedience, whether you like it or not. Stamp out your self-centered ways, and rid yourself of your swollen pride. Do not feel superior to anyone, but place yourself at the service of all.

And do not complain. After all, you have offended God so often that you doubtless deserve hell over and over again! But because your soul is precious to me, I have spared you. I have done so in order that you might understand my love and come to be always grateful for the gifts that I give to you. I have done so in order that you might grow in true humility, not being concerned about what others may think of you.

Chapter 14

f Seeing Ourselves through God's Eyes

Disciple:

You thunder your judgments over me, Lord, and all my bones quake with fear and trembling, and my soul is terribly afraid. I stand stunned and consider that the heavens are not pure in your sight. If you found corruption in the angels and did not spare them, what will happen to me? The stars of heaven fell, and what can I, who am but dust, think will happen to me? Those whose works seemed praiseworthy have fallen to the depths, and I see those who ate the bread of angels delighting in pig slop!

There is no holiness, Lord, if you withdraw your hand, no wisdom if you cease to govern, no courage if you cease to save, no chastity if you do not protect it, no watchfulness if your holy vigilance is missing. If you abandon us, we sink and perish, but if you visit us, we are raised up and live. Why, we are trembling, but through you we are strengthened; we are lukewarm, but by you we are set ablaze.

Oh, how humbly and lowly I ought to feel about myself, and even if I seem to have goodness, I ought to think nothing of it. Oh, how deeply I ought to submit myself to your unfathomable judgments, Lord, where I find myself to be nothing but nothing, absolutely nothing. O measureless weight! O impassable sea! I peer deep within myself and I find nothing but total nothingness.

So where can pride hide? Where is confidence born of virtue? All empty boasting is swallowed up in the depths of your judgments over me. What am I—or any of us—in your sight? Shall the clay boast against he who formed it? How can a person whose heart is truly in harmony with God become swollen with pride? If your whole hope were fixed on God, and if you were to live your whole life for him alone, nothing in this world could inflate your pride or flatter your vanity. All those whose smooth tongues speak empty praise are nothing in themselves, for they will fade away with the sound of their own voices, but the truth of the Lord endures forever.

Chapter 15

f What We Are to Do and Say about All Our Desires

Jesus:

My friend, speak about everything in this way: "Lord, if it is pleasing to you, let this be done. Lord, if it is to your honor, let this be done in your name. Lord, if you see that it will help me and if you judge it to be useful, then grant me this to use for your honor. But if you know it to be harmful for me and of no help in saving my soul, then take this desire away from me."

Not every desire is from the Holy Spirit, even though it may seem right and good to a person at the time. It is hard to tell just what is urging you on to want this thing or that. Many people are fooled in the end who at the beginning seemed led by a good inspiration. Therefore, whatever comes into your head as something you want, ask for it always with reverence toward God and with a humble heart. Above all, leave everything to me, saying: "Lord, you know what is best. Let this or that be done as you wish. Give what you want, how much you want and when you want. Do with me as you think best and as best pleases you and in a way which will give you greater honor. Put me where you want me and use me freely. I am in your hand; turn me around whichever way you will. See! I am your servant, ready for anything. Since it is so, I do not wish to live for myself, but for you. Would that I could live only for you, fittingly and flaw-lessly!"

Disciple:

Prayer that God's Will Be Done

Most kind Jesus, grant me your grace so that it may be with me and work with me and remain with me to the end. Grant me this: always to desire and to want what is most ac-ceptable and pleasing to you. Let your will be mine, and let my will always follow yours and be in perfect accord with it. Let what I want always be what you want, and let me not want anything that you do not want.

Grant that nothing in the world might be as important to me as you are, and for your sake grant that I may serve you with deep humility and love, caring little for recognition or honor. Grant above all else, that I may rest in you and that my heart may find peace in you. You are the heart's true peace; you are its only rest. Apart from you everything is hard and uneasy. Only in this peace that is you, highest and eternal Good, do I find sleep and take my rest. Amen.

Chapter 16

 hat We Are to Seek True Comfort in God Alone

Disciple:

Whatever comfort I can desire or imagine I do not look for here but in the life to come, for if I had all the world's comforts all to myself and could enjoy all its pleasures, they would certainly not last very long. So, my soul, you cannot be fully comforted nor perfectly refreshed except in God, the consoler of the poor and the protector of the humble.

Wait a little, my soul, wait for the divine promise, and you will have more than enough of all good things in heaven. If your appetite for present things is excessive you may lose eternal and heavenly ones. Use the things of the world, but long for the things of eternity. You cannot be fully satisfied by material possessions, for you are simply not made to enjoy them. Even if you owned every good thing in the world you would not be happy and blessed, for your blessedness and joy is in God, who created all those things. Your happiness is not in what is seen and admired by others but in what the good and faithful followers of Christ seek. Your happiness is in what the spiritual and pure of heart, those whose citizenship is in heaven, sometimes experience in this life, though it is meant for the next.

All human solace is empty and brief; blessed and true is that comfort which is acquired within from truth itself. A devout person carries Jesus, his consoler, with him everywhere and says to him: "Be with me, Lord Jesus, in all places and at all times. Let this be my consolation: to be willing to lack all human comfort, and if your consolation is also taken away, then let your will and the just trial you send me be my greatest comfort, for you will not always chide me nor will you keep your anger forever."

Chapter 17

hat We Should Take All Our Cares to God

Jesus:

My dear friend, let me do with you as I will; I know what is best for you. You think in human terms; in many instances you let your feelings affect your decisions.

Disciple:

Lord, what you say is true. Your concern for me is greater than any concern that I can have for myself. A person stands exposed to chance who does not cast all his cares on you. Lord, as long as my will remains firm and strong toward you, do with me whatever pleases you, for whatever you do with me cannot be other than good. If you want me to be in darkness, may you be blessed, and if you want me to be in light, may you still be blessed. If you choose to comfort me, may you be blessed, and if you want me to be troubled, may you be blessed just the same.

Jesus:

My dear friend, this is how you must be if you wish to walk with me: You must be as ready to suffer as to rejoice; you must be as willing to be poor and needy as to be rich and wealthy.

Disciple:

Lord, I shall freely suffer for you whatever you choose to come upon me. With equal readiness I wish to receive from your hand good and evil, sweet and bitter, joy and sorrow, and I wish to thank you for all that happens to me. Guard me from all sin, and I shall fear neither death nor hell. As long as you do not cast me off forever, nor blot me from the book of life, whatever trials come over me shall not harm me.

Chapter 18

hat We Should Bear Our Hardships Patiently after Christ's Example

Jesus:

My dear friend, I came down from heaven to save you. I took your troubles upon myself not because I had to, but because I was drawn by love. I did so in order that you might learn patience and bear life's miseries without complaint. From the hour of my birth until my death on the cross I was never without sorrow. I sadly lacked the material things of this world. I often heard many complaints against me. I meekly endured anxiety and shame. For my kindness I received ingratitude; for my miracles, blasphemies; and for my teaching, rebukes.

Disciple:

Lord, because you were patient during your lifetime, in this perfectly fulfilling your Father's command, it is right that I, a poor sinner, should patiently put up with myself according to your will. As long as it pleases you, I should bear the burdens of this life for my salvation, for although this present life feels heavy, it already has been made deeply worthwhile through your grace. By your example and the footsteps of your saints, life has become more bearable and understandable. It has also become much more comforting than in times past under the Old Law when the gate of heaven was kept shut and the road to heaven seemed hidden and when so few cared to seek the kingdom of heaven. In any case, those who were destined to be saved in those days could not enter the kingdom of heaven before your suffering and the obligation of your holy death.

Oh, how many thanks must I give to you for kindly stooping to show to me and to all the faithful the straight and good road into your eternal kingdom! For your life is our path, and by holy patience we walk to you, our crown. If you had not gone before us and taught us the way, who would have taken the trouble to follow? Alas! how many people would have lingered far behind unless they had seen your splendid example? Look at us! Many people are still indifferent after hearing of your wonders and teachings. What would happen if we did not have such a light to follow?

Chapter 19

f Bearing Injuries and the Proof of True Patience

Jesus:

What are you saying, my friend? Stop complaining, and think of my Passion and the suffering of the other saints. You have not yet shed blood in the fight. Your suffering is little compared to those who suffered so much, who were strongly tempted, grievously afflicted, tried and harassed in so many ways. You must, therefore, call to mind the heavier trials of others so that you may bear your little ones more easily. And if they do not seem small to you, be careful that this is not due to your impatience. But whether they are small or great, try to bear them with patience.

The better you prepare yourself for suffering, the more wisely will you act and the more merit will you gain. You will find it easier, too, if your mind has been prepared for it and is used to it. Do not say: "I cannot tolerate these things from such a man nor should I have to put up with them. He has seriously hurt me and he has blamed me for things I never dreamed of doing. I shall gladly suffer reasonable criticism from someone else, though." Such a thought is foolish, for it does not take into account the virtue of patience nor him from whom patience will receive its reward. Instead, it dwells on personalities and the injuries they inflict.

He is not a truly patient person who is only willing to suffer as much as he chooses and from whom he pleases. The truly patient person does not care by whom he is tried, whether by his superior or by someone equal or inferior, whether by a good and holy person or by a perverse and worthless one. No matter how much or how often anything bad happens to him, and whatever creature in this world might be its cause, he takes it all from God's hand gratefully and considers it a great gain, for nothing suffered for God's sake, no matter how small it may be, goes without its reward.

So be prepared to fight if you want to have the victory. You cannot gain the crown of patience without a struggle. If you will not suffer, you refuse to be crowned, but if you want to be crowned, fight bravely and endure patiently. Without labor there is no rest; without struggle there is no victory.

Disciple:

Lord, may grace make possible what my nature seems to make impossible. You know how little I am able to suffer and how quickly I collapse when the slightest adversity rears its head. Let the endurance of any trials become lovely and desirable to me for your name, for suffering and affliction for your sake is most wholesome to my soul.

Chapter 20

f Admitting Our Own Weaknesses

Disciple:

I shall acknowledge my sinfulness to you, Lord; to you I shall confess my weakness. It is often a small thing which troubles and depresses me. I resolve to act bravely, but when a small temptation comes my way

I find myself in great anxiety. Sometimes grave temptation springs from a trifling thing. And when I think myself fairly safe, before I know it, I am almost toppled by a gentle breeze. Therefore, Lord, look on my lowliness and weakness, noted by you on every side. Have pity on me and draw me out of the mire, lest I sink and remain totally submerged.

It is this that often strikes me again and again and embarrasses me in your sight: that I am so unsteady and weak in resisting my passions. And although I may not give in altogether, yet their chasing after me is trying and distressing to me; it is exhausting to live life in a daily quarrel. My weakness is made known to me by this: that abominable fantasies always burst into my mind more easily than they fade from it.

Most mighty God of Israel, zealous lover of faithful souls, look upon the toil and sorrow of your servant, and help him in all he tries to do. Reinforce me with heavenly strength, lest my darker side get the upper hand and take control.

Alas! what kind of life is this where trials and miseries abound, where everything is full of traps and enemies? When one trial or temptation passes, another comes, and even while one conflict rages on, a gaggle of others scurry in from out of nowhere.

How can a life be loved that is filled with so much bitterness, that is subject to so many calamities and miseries? How can it be called life when it gives birth to so many deadly and disastrous things?

Yet loved it is, and many cling to it desperately. Some people say that the world's values are deceptive and hollow, yet these same people do not willingly give them up, for their lives are completely dominated by them. Yet, some things urge us to love the world's values, while others urge us not to. The pursuit of money, power and sex draws us to accept what the world says we should want, but the feeling of emptiness that accompanies getting them often begets a deep aversion to them.

Sadly, though, such values are terribly addictive, and they usually win over a person so completely that he counts it a delight to be caught in a bed of thorns. Such an unfortunate person neither sees nor tastes the sweetness of God, nor does he know the inner beauty of living in harmony with God's will. Those who strive to live their lives for God, though, see all too clearly how mistaken and deluded the world is and in how many ways it fools itself.

Chapter 21

hat We Should Rest in God above All Else

Disciple:

O my soul, above all things and in all things always rest in the Lord, for he is the eternal rest of the saints.

Grant me most sweet and loving Jesus, to rest in you above every other creature, above all health and beauty, above all glory and honor, above all power and dignity, above all knowledge and precise thought, above all wealth and talent, above all joy and exultation, above all fame and praise, above all sweetness and consolation, above all hope and promise, above all merit and desire, above all gifts and favors you give and shower upon me, above all happiness and joy that the mind can understand and feel, and finally, above all angels and archangels, above all the hosts of heaven, above all things visible and invisible, and above all that is not you, my God.

You, O Lord, my God, you are supreme above all things. You alone are most high, you alone are most powerful, you alone are self-sufficient and complete, you alone are most sweet and delightful, you alone are most beautiful and loving, you alone are most noble and glorious above all things. In you all good exists perfectly and at once; it always was and it always will be. Therefore, whatever you give me, other than yourself, or whatever you reveal or promise to me is far too little, is not enough, as long as I do not see you or fully embrace you. My heart cannot truly rest nor be fully content, if it does not rise above all gifts and all created things and rest in you.

O my most beloved spouse, Jesus Christ, most pure lover, Lord of all creation, who will give me the wings of true freedom to fly to you and to rest in you? Oh, when shall I be free to see how sweet you are, my Lord God? When shall I find myself so completely absorbed in you that for love of you I shall not be conscious of myself but of you alone, beyond all ability to understand or to measure and in a way unique to me?

But now I often lament and bear my unhappiness with a heavy heart, for many evils befall me in this valley of tears. They often upset me, sadden me and cast a dark shadow over me. They often get in the way and distract me, allure and entangle me, so that I cannot freely come to you nor enjoy the happy embraces that always await the blessed spirits.

Let my sighs and great loneliness upon this earth move you, O Jesus, splendor of eternal glory, comfort of the wandering soul. My mouth falls silent before you; my silence speaks to you. How long will my Lord delay in coming? Let him come to me, his poor servant, and make me happy. Let him stretch forth his hand and deliver me from all distress, I who am so greatly in need of compassion.

Come, come. Without you no day or hour will be happy, for you are my joy, and without you my table is empty. I am miserable. I am as one imprisoned and loaded down with heavy chains until you revive me with the light of your presence and set me free and turn your kind face upon me. Others may go their own way, but nothing else delights me nor shall delight me except you, my God, my hope and my eternal salvation. I shall not be silent nor will I cease to pray until your grace returns to me and you speak to me in the depths of my heart.

Jesus:

My dear friend, I am here. See, I have come to you because you have invited me. Your tears and your soul's longing, your humility and your grief-stricken heart have moved me and brought me to you.

Disciple:

O Lord, I called you and longed to enjoy you, and I am prepared to give up everything for you. You first inspired me to seek you; therefore, may you be blessed, Lord, you who have granted this favor to your servant, according to your abundant mercy. What more does your servant have to say in your presence except that he should humble himself before you, remembering always his own shortcomings and unworthiness? There is no one like you among all the wonders of heaven and earth. Your works are exceedingly good, your judgments are true, and by your providence you govern the universe. Praise, therefore, and glory to you, O Wisdom of the Father. Let my mouth, my soul and all creation praise and bless you.

Chapter 22

f Remembering God's Many Blessings

Disciple:

Lord, open my heart to your law, and teach me to walk according to your ways. Help me to understand your will, and with great reverence and diligent thought help me to keep in mind your kindnesses, both those given to everyone and those given especially to me, so that from now on I may suitably thank you. I know well and I fully admit that I am unable to offer you the praise and thanks that I ought, even for the least of your blessings. I am unworthy of any of the good things you have bestowed on me. When I consider your excellence my spirit wilts before your greatness.

All that we have in soul and in body and whatever outward or inward, natural or supernatural qualities we possess, they are your blessings and they celebrate your bounty, mercy, and goodness; from you we have received all good things. And if one person receives more and another less, yet all are yours, and without you we cannot have even the smallest of them.

One who has received more should not boast of his own merit nor lift himself above others nor look down on those having less, for he is a greater and better person who attributes less to himself, and he is all the more humble and devout in returning thanks. The person who always views himself humbly is the more fit to receive greater things.

One who has received less ought not to become dejected nor indignant nor envy the someone who has received more. Instead, he should turn to you and greatly praise your goodness, because you bestow your gifts so abundantly, so willingly, so freely, without considering a person's rank or worth. Everything comes from you, and so you must be praised in everything. You know what is best to give to each of us. Why this person has less and that person has more is not our business but yours. You alone know each person's merits.

For that reason, Lord God, I consider it a great blessing not to have many of those things that in other's eyes might appear praiseworthy and wonderful, for anyone who reflects on his own poverty and lowliness may not feel a burden or sadness or dejection in it but a comfort and a great joy. You, O God, have chosen the poor and humble and those who are despised by the world to be your friends and members of your household. Your Apostles, whom you have made princes over all the earth, are themselves witnesses to this. They lived in the world without complaint, so lowly and simple, so without malice or deceit that they were even happy to suffer insults for your name, and with great affection they embraced what most of the world detests.

Nothing, therefore, ought so to delight one who loves you and knows your kindnesses than that your will and your eternal purposes be accomplished in him. He ought to be as content and happy in being considered the least of all as another is in being thought the greatest. He enjoys as much peace and contentment in the last place as in the first. He is as cheerful being ignored and rejected, devoid of name and reputation, as another is when he is thought to be full of honor and greatness.

Your will and the love of your honor ought to take first place above all else. They should please and comfort a person better than all the blessings which one has or ever will have.

Chapter 23

f Four Things that Bring Great Peace

Jesus:

My dear friend, now I shall teach you the way of peace and true freedom.

Disciple:

Do as you say, Lord, for this I delight to hear!

Jesus:

Strive, my friend, to do another's will rather than your own; always prefer to have less than more; always seek the lower place and be submissive in all things; always wish and pray that God's will may be entirely fulfilled in you, for you see, the person who does all this enters a place of peace and rest.

Disciple:

Lord, this brief talk of yours is full of perfection. It has few words, but it is rich in meaning and abundant in reward. If I could faithfully keep your words, I should not so easily be upset, for as often as I feel myself uneasy or burdened, I find that I have strayed from this teaching. But you who can accomplish all things and always care for my soul's good, grant me greater grace so that I can put into practice your words and achieve my salvation.

A Prayer Against Evil Thoughts

O Lord, my God, do not be far from me; O my God, hasten to help me, for a multitude of evil thoughts have risen up against me and great fears trouble my soul. How shall I pass through them unharmed? How shall I shatter them?

Jesus:

I shall go before you and bring down the braggarts of the earth. I shall open the prison doors and reveal to you the most hidden secrets.

Disciple:

Lord, do as you say, and let all evil thoughts disappear before your face. This is my hope and my only consolation: to fly to you in every affliction, to confide in you, to call upon you from the depths of my being, and patiently to await your solace.

A Prayer for the Mind's Enlightenment

Good Jesus, enlighten me with the clear shining of inner light, and expel all darkness from the chambers of my heart. Restrain my many wandering thoughts, and crush the temptations that batter me. Fight strongly for me, and conquer the wicked beasts—I mean those seductive, sensual urgings of mine—so that peace may be gained through your power and so that your praise may resound fully in your holy temple—that is, in a pure conscience.

Command the winds and storms; say to the sea, "Be still," and to the north wind, "Do not blow," and there will be a great calm. Send forth your light and your truth that they may shine upon the earth, for until you enlighten me I am an empty and vacant land. Pour forth your grace from above; water my heart with heavenly dew; send down the waters of devotion to irrigate the face of the earth so that it may bear good and perfect fruit. Lift up my mind, oppressed by the weight of sins, and raise my every longing to heavenly heights, so that having tasted the sweetness of a higher happiness I may be ashamed to think of mundane things. Take me away and deliver me from the fleeting comforts of all material things, for no material thing can fully satisfy me, comfort me or console me. Unite me to yourself with an unbreakable bond of love, for you alone can satisfy one who loves you.

Without you everything else is pointless.

Chapter 24

f Avoiding Curiosity about Other People's Lives

Jesus:

My friend, do not be inquisitive nor burden yourself with useless things. What is this or that affair to you? Your duty is to follow me. What does it matter to you whether this person is so and so or whether that one says such and such? You will not have to answer for others, but you will have to answer for yourself. So, why get involved?

Look, I know everyone, and I see everything that is done under the sun. I know how it is with each and every person—what he thinks, what he wants and what he has set his sights upon. So, everything should be left to me. As for you, keep yourself in good peace, and let the busybody fuss to his heart's content, for whatever he might do or say will return to haunt him. No one can deceive me.

Do not fall all over yourself in an effort to bask in the shadow of famous people nor to have a pack of acquaintances nor to enjoy the personal affection of a few close friends. These things breed distractions and great darkness in the heart. I would willingly speak to you and reveal my most inner thoughts if you would carefully await my coming and open the door of your heart to me. Be prudent, watch in prayer, and be humble in all things.

Chapter 25

O f True Peace of Heart

Jesus:

My dear friend, I have said: "I leave you peace, my peace I give you; the peace that I give is not the peace that the world gives." Everyone wants peace, but not all care for what leads to true peace. My peace is with the humble and gentle of heart; your peace will be in exercising great patience. If you hear me and follow my voice, you will enjoy great peace.

Disciple:

So, what shall I do?

Jesus:

In all things consider well what you do and what you say, and direct everything you hope to do to this end: that you please only me and desire and seek nothing but me. As to what others say or do, pass no flip judgments, and do not entangle yourself in things that do not concern you. Follow this advice and you will seldom be troubled. Yet, keep in mind that never to feel any disquiet nor to suffer any heartache or physical pain is not the stuff of this present life, but of eternity.

So, do not believe that you have found real peace if you feel no burden nor that all is well if you suffer no opposition. And do not assume everything to be perfect if things seem to be going your way. Neither should you consider yourself something great or especially beloved by God if you happen to enjoy great devotion and tenderness. A true lover of virtue is not known by such things as this nor does your progress and perfection consist of such things.

Disciple:

Of what, then, do they consist, Lord?

Jesus:

They consist of offering yourself with your whole heart to the will of God, in not seeking your own interests in things great or small, in time or eternity, so that with one steady outlook through prosperity and adversity, weighing everything in the same balance, you will continue to be grateful.

If your hope can be so strong and so steadfast that when inner comfort seems to disappear, you can even then prepare your heart for greater onslaughts, then you will find true peace. If you are not so self-righteous as to think that you should not have to suffer hardships, then you will find true joy. And if you thank me just the same both in comfort and in trial, then you will know that I am truly present in your life. When you achieve such a complete disregard for your own self-importance, then you will find as much peace as it is possible to have in this present life.

Chapter 26

hat True Freedom Comes More from Humble Prayer than from Much Reading

Disciple:

Lord, this is the work of a perfect person: never to allow the soul to relax from straining after heavenly things and to pass among the many cares of this world as though they did not exist, not in an apathetic way, but with a freedom that comes from loving you above all else. My most gracious Lord, I implore you to keep me from the cares of this life, lest I find myself entangled in them; from the body's many wants, lest I become enslaved to them; from every obstacle of the soul, lest I break under the anxiety and utterly collapse.

I do not ask that you deliver me from those things which people in their vanity so feverishly chase after. I only ask that you free me from those ills which accompany our mortality and that painfully weigh me down and keep me from experiencing your presence as often as I would like.

O God, my unutterable sweetness, turn into bitterness for me every comfort that draws me from the love of eternal things and wrongly entices me to itself under the guise of some present, delightful good. Do not let it overcome me, O my God; do not let the world with its values deceive me and win me over. Do not let the devil and his cunning trip me up. Give me strength to resist, patience to suffer and constancy to keep on. Give the anointing of your spirit in place of all worldly rewards, and in place of self-centeredness, fill me with the love of your name.

Look and see how food, drink, clothes and other things needed to support me are burdensome when I burn with love for you. Allow me to use such things sparingly and not to be caught up in wanting them too much. We are not allowed to reject them all, for nature must be sustained, but your holy law forbids us to ask for more than we need and for things that mainly prop up our self-importance. If we do, we feel endless conflict.

In all this I ask that your hand may guide me and lead me that I may never yield to excess.

Chapter 27

hat Self-love Blocks Us from Attaining the Highest Good

Jesus:

My dear friend, you must give all to get all, and nothing of yourself is to remain. Know that self-love hurts you more than anything else in the world. Everything clings to you more or less according to the love and affection that you have for it. If your love is pure, simple and good, you will not be a slave to anything. Do not lust after things you should not have. Do not possess what will possess you. It surprises me that with all you can wish for and all you can have, you have not wished for me from the very depths of your heart.

Why do you pine away with empty grief? Why wear yourself out with needless cares? Continue to please me and nothing will harm you. If you seek this thing or that, or if you want to be in this place or that because it will be more profitable or pleasing to you, you will never find peace. In everything you will find something wrong, and everywhere you go, you will find someone you won't like.

Acquiring and storing up possessions is of no help either; rather, being indifferent to them and cutting them from your heart will help the most. This, you understand, applies not only to money and wealth but to the drive for honor and the desire for praise, all of which mean nothing in the end.

Having an important position in your community means nothing either if you lack a loving heart, nor will the peace that you seek last for long if your heart is not rooted in its proper soil. Without me you can change, but you may not be any better for it. When the opportunity for recognition and self-importance arises—and you take it—then you run into what you tried to avoid—and more.

Disciple:

A Prayer for a Clean Heart and Heavenly Wisdom

Strengthen me, O God, by the grace of the Holy Spirit. Make my inner self strong, and empty my heart of all useless anxiety and distress. May I not be drawn away by conflicting desires, be they worthless or prized, but may I consider them all as passing things and I too as passing with them. Nothing under the sun is lasting here where all is vanity and vexation of spirit. Oh, how wise is the person who thinks this way!

Give me, O Lord, heavenly wisdom that more than anything else I may learn to seek and to find you, to taste and to love you above all things, and to understand all other things as they are, as your wisdom has ordained them to be. Give me discretion to avoid those who puff me up with flattery and the patience to bear with those who work against me. It is great wisdom not to be tossed thither and yon by windy words nor to give ear to the falsely flattering serpent. May we each go confidently along the path he has started!

Chapter 28

f Those Who Speak against Us

Jesus:

My dear friend, do not take it to heart if some people think ill of you and say things about you that you would rather not hear. You should think worse of yourself and believe that no one is weaker than you are. If you walk by an inner light, you will not think much of words that are hurled at you. It is no little discretion to be silent in bad times, to turn inwardly to me, and not to be upset by what other people think.

Your peace does not depend on what other people say; whether they think well or ill of you, you remain the same person. Where is true peace and true glory? Is it not in me? The person who has no wish to please others—nor who is afraid to displease them—will enjoy great peace. All unquietness of heart and distracted thought springs from having too great a love for the wrong things—and from needless fear.

Chapter 29

f How We Should Bless God in Times of Trial

Disciple:

Blessed be your name forever, O Lord, for you have willed this trial and temptation to come upon me. I cannot escape it, but must fly to you so that you may help me and turn it to my good.

Lord, I am in great distress even as we speak, and my heart is distraught. My present suffering overwhelms me. And now, my Lord, what am I to say? I am in dire straights. Save me from this hour! Yet, I came to this hour for only one reason: that you might be glorified when I shall have been deeply humbled and set free by you. May it please you, O Lord, to deliver me, poor person that I am, for what can I do and where can I go without you?

Give me patience, Lord, even in this misfortune. Help me, O my God, and I shall not be afraid, no matter how much I may be oppressed. And now, in the midst of these things, what shall I say? Lord, your will be done! I have certainly deserved to be troubled and burdened. I must bear it at all costs, and may it be with patience until the storm passes over and things get better.

Yet, your almighty hand has the power to remove this temptation from me and to lessen its force lest I sink under it, as you have done so often for me in the past, my God, my mercy. The harder it is for me to fight off these temptations, the easier it is for the right hand of the Most High to turn things in the proper direction.

Chapter 30

f Asking for God's Help

Jesus:

My dear friend, I am the Lord who gives strength in the day of affliction. Come to me in times of trouble. The main thing that gets in the way of heavenly comfort is that you are slow in turning to prayer. Before you finally settle down for a serious talk with me, you look for all sorts of other comforts and you try to recover your spirits by keeping busy. So, it comes to pass that none of it helps very much until you remember that I am the one who rescues those who trust in me. Outside of me, there is no effective help, no worthwhile advice, no lasting cure.

But now that the storm is over and you have caught your breath, grow strong again in the light of my mercies, for I am close at hand to restore everyone, and to restore them abundantly and beyond measure.

Is anything impossible for me? Shall I be like one who breaks a promise? Where is your faith? Stand firmly and persevere. Be patient and have courage. Comfort will come to you in due time. Wait for me. Wait. I shall come and heal you. It is temptation that vexes you and needless fear that frightens you. What does anxiety about the future bring but sorrow upon sorrow? Today has troubles enough of its own. It is vain and useless to feel either grief or joy about future things that perhaps may never happen.

But it is human to be fooled by such imaginings, and to the extent that one is easily drawn away by the suggestions of the enemy, it is a clear sign that the soul is still weak. The enemy does not care whether it be with true or false things that he abuses and deceives you, or whether he overcomes you with the love of present things or the fear of future ones.

So, do not let your heart be troubled and do not be afraid. Believe in me and trust in my mercy. When you think yourself far from me, I am often closest to you. When you think that almost everything is lost, then often you are about to gain the greatest reward. All is not lost when things do not turn out the way you planned. You must not judge according to the way you feel now nor get so lost in your troubles that it seems there is no way out. Do not think yourself totally abandoned, though for the time being I have sent you some affliction or taken from you the comfort that you want. This is the road to the kingdom of heaven. Doubtless, it is better for you—and for the rest of my servants—that you be tried by adversities than that you have everything turn out the way you would like.

I know your innermost thoughts, and I know that it is more helpful for your salvation that you should sometimes be left feeling flat and spiritually listless. If you always felt aglow with love and full of joy, you would soon become proud of your good fortune and pleased with yourself, thinking yourself to be something you are not. What I have given I can take away, and I can return it when I please. When I give it, it is still mine; when I take it away, I do not take what is yours, for every good gift and every perfect gift is mine. If I send you affliction or adversity, neither complain nor lose heart. I can quickly lift you up again and turn all your trouble into joy.

In all this, I am just, and I am to be highly commended when I deal with you in such a way. If you understand the truth and face it squarely, you should never feel let down or depressed when things go wrong; rather, you should rejoice and give thanks. Yes, you should even consider it a special joy that in sending you sorrows I do not spare you.

"As the Father has loved me, so I love you," I said to my beloved disciples, whom I certainly did not send out to a good time, but to a great battle; not to honors, but to scorn; not to idleness, but to work; not to rest, but to bear much fruit through hardship. O my beloved friend, remember these words!

Chapter 31

f Setting Aside All Created Things that We May Find the Creator

Disciple:

Lord, I need an even greater grace if I am to progress so far in the spiritual life that neither other people nor any other thing can stand in my way, for as long as anything holds me back I am not free to fly to you. That person wished to fly freely who said: "Who will give me wings like a dove's that I may fly away and find rest?" Who is more at rest than he whose sight is simple, fixed on God alone? And who is more free than the person who desires nothing but God?

A person should, therefore, soar beyond every created thing, leave his self-importance completely behind, and stand enrapt to see that you, the Creator of all, have no equal in your creation. And unless one were cut loose from clinging to created things, one could not freely attend to spiritual things. This is why there are so few contemplative men and women today: Very few people know how to let everything they do in this world flow from their love for God.

A great grace is needed for this, which may lift the soul and carry it above itself. Unless a person is lifted up in spirit, is cut loose from worldly values, and is wholly united to God, whatever he knows and whatever he has mean nothing. Anyone who considers anything to be great, except the One, the immeasurable and eternal Good, will always be a small person, tied to the earth. Whatever is not God is nothing by comparison and should be recognized as such.

There is a vast difference between the wisdom of an enlightened and devout person and the knowledge of a well-read and accomplished scholar. The learning that flows from divine influence is far more noble than that acquired by a person's study and research.

Many people wish for the contemplative life, but they do not practice those things necessary to attain it. One great obstacle is that they rely on signs and feelings and have little concern about doing away with their own self-centeredness. I do not know what it is or what we think we are doing that we, who claim to be so spiritual, so seldom give any thought to our inner lives. I do not know what spirit leads us to take such great pains and to be so apprehensive about passing and petty things. What a pity that after a brief recollection we rush off without rigorously examining our behavior. We pay no attention to where our affections lie nor do we deplore how impure they all are. It was because we had become corrupt that the great flood followed; therefore, since our hearts are corrupt, it follows that the actions flowing from them should also be corrupt. It shows that we lack inner commitment and vitality. From a pure heart flows a good life.

We ask how much a person has accomplished in life, but we do not weigh his virtues so earnestly. We ask whether he is strong, rich, handsome, talented, a good writer, a good singer, or a good worker, but few of us ask how poor in spirit, how patient and kind, or how devout and inward he is. Nature looks at a person's outward appearance, but grace looks inside; nature is often mistaken, but grace never is, since it trusts in God.

Chapter 32

Of Growing beyond Self

Jesus:

My friend, you cannot have perfect freedom unless you stop being so self-centered—and unless you stop it once and for all. All those who are so caught up in themselves are chained like slaves; they rush in circles, chase every whim, and always seek the easy path, not the path of Jesus Christ. Nothing that such a person plans or accomplishes will last, for everything that does not come from God will perish. Remember this short and meaningful saying: "Forsake all and you will find all; give up your desires and you will find rest.'' Ponder this, and when you have put it into practice you will understand everything.

Disciple:

Lord, this is not one day's work nor is it child's play. This brief saying contains everything a religious person must strive for.

Jesus:

Dear friend, you should not give up nor lose heart when you hear what the way of perfection is; rather, you should be inspired all the more to reach greater heights—or at least to yearn for them. I wish it were so with you and that you had reached that point at which you were no longer enamored of yourself but stood ready to do my will. Then you would greatly please me and your whole life would pass in happiness and peace.

You still have much to give up, and unless you give it all up for me, holding nothing back, you will not get what you ask for. I urge you to buy from me heavenly wisdom, more valuable than the purest gold, that you may be rich in the things that count. Put aside earthly wisdom and the wish to please others and yourself. I have said to strive for those things that few people value rather than those things that they all clamor for.

True heavenly wisdom seems worthless to most, and it is largely ignored, for it does not think highly of itself nor does it seek greatness in this world. Many pay lip service to it, but they do not practice what they preach. Yet, this same heavenly wisdom is the pearl of great price hidden from the crowd.

Chapter 33

f Our Changing Hearts, and of Focusing Our Sight on God

Jesus:

My friend, do not trust the way you feel at the moment, for your feelings will soon change. All your life you are subject to change, even if you do not want to be. Sometimes you are happy, sometimes you are sad; sometimes you are calm, sometimes restless; now full of devotion, now not; now studious, now lazy; now solemn, now lighthearted.

The person who is wise and well instructed in spiritual things is above these changes, not paying attention to his own feelings or to which way the wind blows. Instead, he directs his full attention toward reaching his desired goal. By focusing his sight on me as he is buffeted to and fro, his feet remain firmly planted. And the more intently he focuses his sight on me, the more steadily he presses on through the changing storm.

But in many people this precise focus is blurred, for they gawk about at any pleasant thing that happens along. Rarely will you find anyone unblemished by mixed feelings. Thus Jesus's countrymen came to Martha and Mary in Bethany, not so much to see Jesus as to see Lazarus. So your focus must be sharp and accurate. It must be directed at me and not be distracted by anything else.

Chapter 34

hat the Person Who Loves God Enjoys Him above All and in All

Disciple:

My God and my all! What more can I want? What greater happiness can I desire? O Words! You are tasty and sweet to those who love you but dry and stale to those who do not. My God and my all! Those words say enough to one who understands, but to one who loves, they are delightful to repeat over and over again.

When you are present, Lord, everything is joyful; when you are missing, everything is dreary. You make the heart calm and full of great peace and gladness. You make us think well of all things and praise you in all things. Nothing can give any lasting pleasure without you, for if anything is to be pleasant and appetizing, your grace must be with it, seasoned with the spice of your wisdom. To the person who delights in you, what will not taste right? And what can give any joy to someone who does not delight in you? Those who love the world apart from you know nothing of your wisdom, and those who love others for their own selfish reasons know even less. Loving the world under such terms smacks of vanity; selfishly loving others plants a doomed vine.

But those who follow you truly love the world and others through you. They are indeed wise. God tastes sweet to them, and whatever good they find in God's creation, they refer it all back to you. There is a great difference—indeed, a vast difference—between the distinctive character of the Creator and that of what he has created, between the eternal and the passing, between light and enlightenment.

O eternal Light, surpassing all created light, send forth a brilliant flash and let it penetrate the most secret recesses of my heart. Cleanse my spirit and give it joy, enlighten it and bring it to life, so that with all its powers it may cling fast to you in boundless joy.

Oh, when will this blessed and desired hour come when you will fill me with your presence and be all in all to me? As long as this is not given to me, my joy will not be complete. But alas! the old man still lives in me. He is not totally nailed to the cross, not fully dead. He still rages against the spirit; he wages war within me and does not allow the kingdom of my soul to be at rest. But you, who rule the power of the sea and calm the surging waves, arise and help me! Scatter the nations that delight in war! Crush them with your power! I beg you, show your wonderful works, and let your right hand be glorified, for there is no other hope or refuge for me but you, O Lord, my God.

Chapter 35

hat There Is No Freedom from Temptation in This Life

Jesus:

My friend, you are never safe in this life. As long as you live you will always need spiritual weapons. You are in the midst of enemies and are attacked right and left. If you do not use the shield of patience, you will not be unwounded for long. What is more, if you do not fix your heart on me with the sincere intention of bearing all things for my sake, you will not be able to withstand the heat of battle nor will you win the victory palm of the blessed. Therefore, you must go through it all courageously and use a strong hand against the enemy, for the food of angels is given to the victor and much misery to the slacker.

If you seek rest in this life, how do you expect to come to eternal rest? Do not make frequent rest your goal but great patience. Seek true peace not on earth but in heaven, not in people or things but in God alone. You should be willing to endure all things for the love of God. Certainly, you should willingly endure labor and sorrows, temptations, vexations, anxieties, necessities, illnesses, injuries, contradictions, rebukes, humiliations, doubts, chastisements and contempt. These things are all aids to virtue; these test one who has begun to follow Christ; these mold a heavenly crown. I pay an infinite wage for a short time at work, and I offer eternal glory for a moment's anxiety.

Do you think you will always have spiritual comforts whenever you please? My saints did not always have them. They met with many troubles and temptations and frequent disappointments; but they patiently endured in all things and showed greater confidence in God than in themselves, knowing that the suffering of this present life is nothing compared to the glory that is to come. Would you expect to have at once what others have received only after many tears and great effort? Wait for the Lord; be strong and take courage. Do not despair or give up, but be constant in offering both body and soul for the glory of God. I shall reward you abundantly. I shall be with you in every trial.

Chapter 36

That You Should Not Worry
about What Other People May Say about You

Jesus:

My dear friend, cast your heart firmly on the Lord, and if your conscience confirms your devotion and innocence, you will not be afraid of anything that others may have to say against you. It is good and blessed to put up with such things, and it will not be too difficult for a person of humble heart who has greater trust in God than in himself. Since many people like to gossip, few pay any attention to them. In any case, it is impossible to satisfy everyone.

Although Paul tried to please everyone in the Lord and became all things to all people, yet he did not think very much of other people's opinions. He worked hard for the edification and salvation of others with all the talent and ability in him. But this did not prevent him from sometimes being judged or despised by them. So, he turned it all over to God, who knows all, and he patiently and humbly defended himself against those who spoke unfairly of him or who thought him deceitful or in error or who hurled insults at him. He sometimes did respond more strongly to their accusations, though, so that those who did not fully understand his actions would not be led astray by them.

Why should you be afraid of what others have to say? Today a person is, and tomorrow he is gone. Love God, and you will not fear others. What can another person's words or shabby treatment do to you? Such people hurt themselves more than they hurt you, and they cannot escape God's judgment, no matter who they are. Keep your eyes fixed on God; do not fight words with words, and if at the moment you seem to be beaten and to suffer an undeserved defeat, do not worry about it, and do not lessen your reward in heaven by losing your temper. Instead, raise your eyes to me in heaven. I can deliver you from every embarrassment and wrong, and I can repay each person according to what he has done.

Chapter 37

f Gaining a Free Heart through Total Self-surrender

Jesus:

My dear friend, abandon yourself, and you will find me. Give up your will and every title to yourself, and you will always come out ahead, for greater grace will be yours the moment you turn yourself over to me once and for all.

Disciple:

Lord, how often shall I resign myself, and in what ways am I to abandon myself?

Jesus:

Do so always and at all times, in small things as in great. I make no exceptions, but wish to find you stripped of everything. How else can we belong to each other unless you are stripped of all self-will, both inside and out? The sooner you do this the better, and the more completely and sincerely you do it, the more you will please me and the more you will gain.

There are some who resign themselves, but they attach conditions to it. They do not trust in God completely, so they take pains to provide for themselves just in case. Some offer everything at first, but later, beaten down by temptations, they go back to their old ways and thus make little progress in virtue. People like these will not gain the true freedom of a pure heart nor the grace of a joyful intimacy with me unless they surrender themselves unconditionally and offer themselves as a sacrifice to me each day. Without this total self-surrender a joyful union between us cannot exist, either now or ever.

I have often said this to you, and now I say it again: Walk away from yourself—let go of yourself—and you will enjoy great inner peace. Give all for all, seek nothing, ask for nothing in return, stand purely and without hesitation with me, and you will have me. You will be free in heart, and no darkness will oppress you. Strive for this, pray for this, long for this: that you may be stripped of all your possessions, and being destitute, you may follow the destitute Jesus; that you may die to yourself and live eternally with me. Then all of your vain fancies, evil thoughts and useless worries will disappear. Then all fear will vanish, and true love will grow.

Chapter 38

Of Controlling Our Behavior, and of Running to God in Time of Danger

Jesus:

My dear friend, you should aim diligently at this: that wherever you are and in whatever you do, you should be inwardly free and master of yourself; all things should be subject to you, not you to them. You should be lord and master of your own actions, not a slave or a hired hand. You are to be a free and true person, going on to the destiny and freedom of the sons and daughters of God. Such people stand above present things and look toward eternal ones. With the left eye they see passing things; with the right they see heavenly things. They are not attracted by the things of this world so that they cling to them, but instead they use them as intended by God, the Supreme Artist, who has left nothing without purpose in his creation.

Likewise, no matter what the occasion or event, do not believe everything you see or hear. Instead, do as Moses did. Quickly go into the Tabernacle to confer with the Lord, and you will often hear the divine answer that allows you to return informed about many things, present and future. Moses always had recourse to the Tabernacle for solving doubts and questions, and he ran to prayer for help in easing dangers and in dealing with unscrupulous people.

So you, too, should take refuge in the secret chamber of your heart, and there earnestly ask for divine help. We read that Joshua and the sons of Israel were deceived by the Gibeonites because they did not first consult the Lord. They were too quick to believe sweet-sounding words, and they were soon tricked by flattery.

Chapter 39

hat a Person Must Not Be Overly Eager in His Affairs

Jesus:

My friend, always bring your concerns to me, and I shall take care of them at the proper time. Wait for me to arrange it, and you will see that everything will work out just fine.

Disciple:

Lord, I shall willingly entrust all things to you, for my thoughts on these matters can be of little avail. I wish that I cared less about what might happen in the future and instead could offer myself to you without hesitation.

Jesus:

It often happens that a person vigorously pursues something that he wants, but when he gets it, he begins to feel differently about it. A person's likes and dislikes do not always stay the same but drive him instead from one thing to another. It is therefore of great importance to abandon yourself even in the smallest things. True progress consists of redirecting love from yourself to others, and the person who has done so is extremely free and very secure.

But the old enemy, who is against all that is good, never stops tempting. Day and night he lies in wait to ambush some unsuspecting person and hurl him headlong into ruin. "Watch and pray," says the Lord, "that you do not enter into temptation."

Chapter 40

hat All a Person's Goodness Comes from God, Not from Himself

Disciple:

Lord, what is man that you are mindful of him or the son of man that you visit him? What have we done that you should give us your grace? Lord, how can I complain if you leave me or what can I say if you fail to do what I ask? Surely I may truly think and say this: Lord, without you, I am nothing; I can do nothing; I have nothing of myself that is good. I am flawed in all things, and I always tend to nothing, and unless I am helped and instructed by you in the depths of my being, I become cool and lax.

But you, Lord, are always the same; into eternity you remain always good, just and holy. You do all things well with justness and holiness, and you manage all things wisely. But I, who am more inclined to go backward than forward, constantly drift from one state to the next, for seven seasons wreak havoc over me. Yet, things get better when you reach out your helping hand. Only you, without help from anyone else, can so assist and strengthen me that I no longer look from one thing to the next, but I turn my heart to you and find rest in you alone.

So, if I knew how to put aside all other comfort, either for the sake of devotion or because I felt compelled to seek you—because there is no one else who can comfort me—then I might rightly hope for your grace and rejoice again in your gift of new spiritual comfort.

I thank you, for all things that go well for me come from you. For my part, I am hollow and worthless, a fickle and weak person. What do I have to boast about, then, or why do I wish to be held in high regard? Surely not for my nothingness? Now there is vanity! Such an inflated sense of self is an evil plague, the apex of pride, because it draws us away from true glory and robs us of heavenly grace. As long as a person is pleased with himself, he is displeasing to you, and as long as he gapes after other people's praise, he is deprived of real virtues.

True glory and holy joy are found in glorifying you and not in boasting of one's self; in rejoicing in your name and not in one's own strength; in not finding pleasure in any created thing except for your sake. Let your name be praised, not mine; let your work be extolled, not mine; let your holy name be blessed, and let no one's praise fall on me. You are my glory and the joy of my heart. In you will I be blessed all the day long. As for myself, I shall boast of nothing but my weakness. Let others seek praise from others; I shall seek praise from God alone.

When compared to your eternal glory, all human glory, all temporal honor, all worldly eminence are vain and foolish. O my God, Blessed Trinity, my truth and my mercy, to you alone be praise, honor, power, and glory forever and ever.

Chapter 41

f Seeing All Worldly Honor as Nothing

Jesus:

My dear friend, do not become withdrawn if you see others honored and promoted and yourself looked down upon and humiliated. Lift up your heart to me in heaven and you will not feel so bad.

Disciple:

Lord, we are blind and quickly seduced by vanity. If I closely examine myself, I see that no living creature has ever done me an injury for which I could justly complain against you. But since I have often seriously sinned against you, it is only right that all creation should be armed against me. Confusion and contempt are therefore my just deserts, but praise, honor and glory are due to you.

Unless I prepare myself for this and am willing to be scorned and forsaken by all creation and to be seen as an absolute nobody, I shall never find inner peace and stability nor shall I ever become spiritually enlightened or perfectly at one with you.

Chapter 42

hat Peace Does Not Depend on Other People

Jesus:

My dear friend, if your peace depends only on a mutual love and friendship with another person, your roots will be tangled and shallow. But if you can turn to the ever-living and deeply rooted truth, you will not be grieved when a friend must leave you or when he dies.

The love of a friend should be rooted in me. No matter how good he appears to be or how much you care for him in this life, he should be loved for my sake. Without me, friendship is neither strong nor lasting, nor is it a true and pure love unless I am the bond.

All human affection and friendship is a reflection of the love that I have for you; you should not want any other kind. True friendship is a gift; it takes root in your own heart, and the more you probe its depths, the higher you ascend to God. Friendship is a grace, and it should be nurtured with humility and love. Be thankful for it, and the Holy Spirit will continue to bless you.

Be careful not to let your friendships stand in the way of your love for me. It is easy to place your friends first and God second; looking at created things, it is easy to lose sight of the Creator. In your friendships, as in all other things, always place God first, as the source and font of all that is good.

Chapter 43

gainst Arrogant Learning

Jesus:

My friend, do not let fancy words and artful phrases arouse your interest and curiosity. The kingdom of God is not in words but in power. Listen to my words which kindle hearts and enlighten minds and which bring the sting of conscience and lavishly bestow comfort.

Never read anything just to seem more learned or wise; rather, learn to stamp out your vices, for this will serve you better than knowing the answers to a whole list of hard questions. When you have read and learned many things you have always to come back to the one source. It is I who give knowledge, and it is I who give a clearer understanding to those who are gentle and humble than anyone can teach. The person I speak to will quickly become wise and will progress far in the spiritual life.

But woe to those who spend their lives in rooting out esoteric learning, caring little about how to serve me. The time will come when Christ, the Teacher of teachers, the Lord of angels, will appear to conduct the final exam; that is, to examine each person's conscience. Then he will search Jerusalem with a lamp, and he will bring to light the things hidden in darkness, and all those scholars, so quarrelsome in their learning, will fall silent.

I am he who, in an instant, can raise the humble mind to understand the principles of eternal truth better than anyone who has studied for ten years in graduate school. I teach without the din of words, without the confusion of opinions, without the haughtiness of tenure, without the strife of arguments. I am he who teaches each of you to think little of worldly values, to turn away from popular concerns, to seek everlasting ones, to taste the eternal, to avoid worldly honors, to endure scandal, to put all hope in me, and above all, to love me with a burning, passionate love.

Once there was a person who loved me from the depths of his heart, and he learned divine things, and he spoke of them most wonderfully. He learned more through humility than by studying fine distinctions. To some I speak what is plain to all; to others, what is for them alone. To some I make myself known sweetly in symbol and metaphor; to others, I reveal my mysteries in striking clarity. A book teaches one lesson, but it does not teach everyone equally, for deep within you, I am the Teacher of truth, the Searcher of the heart, the Reader of thoughts, the Mover of deeds, giving understanding to each person as I see fit.

Chapter 44

f Minding Our Own Business

Jesus:

My friend, there are many things in life that you must simply pass by. If you wish to grow in your spiritual life, you must not allow yourself to be caught up in the workings of the world; you must find time alone, away from noise and confusion, away from the allure of power and wealth. You must also turn a deaf ear to many things, and think instead on those things that contribute to your peace. It is better to avert your eyes from what distracts you from your purpose. Quietly leave each person to his own opinion, and avoid contentious bickering. If you stand in good stead with God and respect his ways, you will more easily be able to do this.

Disciple:

O Lord, what have we come to? Just look! We cry a sea of tears over a trivial loss; for a petty gain we scurry about and work our fingers to the bone, and the damage to our soul is soon forgotten—indeed, it is rarely even thought of! We dwell on unimportant things, and we carelessly skip over the most important thing of all. A person's entire being slips into the quicksand of the world, and unless he hoists himself out—and quickly, too—he soon finds himself settled firmly in the mire.

Chapter 45

hat We Should Not Believe Everything We Hear and of How Easy It Is to Speak Ill of Others

Disciple:

Send me your help, Lord, in time of trouble, for help other than yours is no help at all. How often has loyalty turned up missing where I was certain I would find it, and how often have I found it where I least expected it! Looking to others for salvation is foolish; the salvation of the just is in you, O God.

May you be blessed, O Lord, my God, in everything that happens to us. We are weak and unstable, and we quickly make mistakes and change our course. Is there anyone who can behave so carefully and meticulously in everything he does that he never makes mistakes or encounters doubts? But the person who trusts in you, Lord, and who seeks you with a simple heart, does not fall so easily. And if by chance such a person should fall into some trouble—no matter how entangled in it he may become—he will soon be snatched from it or be comforted by you, for right up to the end you will not abandon a person who trusts in you.

It is rare to find a loyal friend who stands by a companion in all his troubles. You, Lord, you alone are most faithful in all things. No one else is like you. Oh, how wise was that holy soul who said: "My mind is firmly set and grounded in Christ." If it were that way with me, human fear would not so easily upset me nor would barbed words provoke me. Who can foresee everything, or who can guard against misfortunes that lie ahead? If the things we expect often hurt us, imagine what those we do not expect can do! Why did I not provide better for myself? And why did I rely so heavily on others? We are only human, after all; we are nothing but frail men and women, even though many think of us as angels and even call us angels!

In whom shall I trust, Lord? In whom but you? You are the Truth who can neither deceive nor be deceived. And in just the opposite way, all of us are prone to falsehood, to being weak, unstable and fickle, especially in what we say. Often we cannot even believe what seems to sound right on the surface, at least not at first. How wisely did you warn us to be careful of what others say, and that a person's enemies are often those of his own household. Even if someone close to us should say, "Look, the Lord is here!" or "Look, the Lord is there!" we should not necessarily believe him.

I have learned my lesson at great expense; may it serve to make me more cautious and not to increase my foolishness. "Be wary," a certain person once said to me, "Be wary. Keep what I say to yourself." And while I am silent and believe the matter to be secret, he himself cannot keep the secret he asked me to keep, but soon he betrays both me and himself, and then he goes on his way! Lord, protect me from all such gossip and from careless people, for I do not want to fall into their hands nor do I want to do as they do. Let me speak only true and honest words; keep me far from crafty rhetoric. What I do not wish to suffer from others, I should certainly avoid doing myself!

Oh, how good and how peaceful it is to keep silent about others and not to believe gossip or spread it around. How good it is to confide in only a few people and to seek you always, the one who probes my heart. How fair it is not to be blown about by the blustery wind of gossip, but to wish that all things, both inside us and out, may be done as you wish. How sure it is for preserving heavenly grace to escape from public show, to avoid causing admiration in others, and to untiringly pursue all those things which better our lives and increase our devotion. How many have been harmed by having their virtue recognized and praised too soon. Indeed, how grace has gained when it was kept hidden during this fragile life, a life which is one test and conflict after another.

Chapter 46

**f Having Confidence in God
when Sharp Words Attack Us**

Jesus:

My dear friend, stand firmly and trust in me, for what are words but words? They fly through the air, but they hurt nothing. If you are at fault, think that you will quickly correct yourself; if your conscience is clear, think that you will freely put up with criticism for God's sake. It is a small enough thing that now and again you must listen to harsh words when you cannot yet endure harsh blows!

And why do such little things go right to your heart, unless you are still rooted in the world and pay more attention to others' opinions than you should? Because you are afraid of being disliked, you are not willing to be criticized for your faults, and so you hide in excuses. But take a good look at yourself, and you will find that you are still full of the world's values and have an empty fondness for pleasing other people. When you refuse to be brought down a few pegs and are upset by your failings, it is as plain as can be that you are not truly humble, that the world is still too much with you. Pay attention to my word and you will not care about ten thousand words that come from others.

Look, if all the things were said against you that the most malicious minds could invent, what harm would it do you if you just let it all pass and considered it to be worth no more than a piece of straw? Could they even so much as pluck one hair from your head? But the person who does not keep his heart within nor God before his eyes is easily annoyed by criticism. The person who trusts in me, though, and who wishes not to stand by his own judgment fears no one, for I am the judge and the knower of all secrets; I understand what happened as it happened; I know the one who inflicts the injury and the one who suffers it. The particular thing said went out through me; it happened by my permission, so that the thoughts of many hearts might be made known. I shall judge the guilty and the innocent, but I wish to try them first in a trial known only to me.

Human evidence often misleads; my judgment is true. It will stand and not be overturned. For the most part it lies hidden and is made known only to a few, yet it is never wrong nor can it ever be wrong, even if it may not seem right in the eyes of some people. Thus, you must run to me in every decision and not depend upon your own judgment. The just person will not be troubled by anything that comes from God. If any unjust charge is spoken against him, he will not much care, neither will he foolishly jump for joy if others find good reason to relieve him of blame. The just person considers that I search the heart and feelings, that I do not judge according to the face of things and how they seem. Often what is full of blame in my eyes is full of praise in yours.

Disciple:

O Lord God, just Judge, strong and patient, who knows the weakness and perversity in others, be my strength and all my confidence, for my own conscience is not enough for me. You know that which I do not know, and so each time that I am criticized I ought to humble myself and bear it meekly. In your mercy, pardon me when I have not done so, and in the future give me grace to endure still more. In obtaining pardon, your abundant mercy is better for me than a self-defense built on my own idea of what I think is right. Although I am not conscious of anything that I have done wrong, yet I cannot justify myself by this, for with your mercy taken away, no living person will be justified in your sight.

Chapter 47

hat All Burdens Are to Be Endured for the Sake of Eternal Life

Jesus:

My friend, do not be ground down by the work you have undertaken for me nor let troubles dishearten you; instead, always let my promise strengthen and console you. I am enough to repay you beyond all limit and measure. You will not labor here for long, nor will you always be burdened with sorrows. Wait a little and you will see a quick end to all your trials. The hour will come when blood, sweat and tears will be no more. All that passes away with time is of little importance, and it passes away quickly.

Whatever you do, do it well; work faithfully in my vineyard, and I shall be your reward. Write, read, sing, mourn, keep silent, pray, bear adversity with courage. Eternal life is worth all these battles—and more. Peace will come on a day that is known only to the Lord, and it will not be a day or night such as we know now, but it will be everlasting light, infinite brightness, steadfast peace, and secure rest. Then you will not say: "Who will deliver me from the body of this death?" Nor will you cry out: "Woe is me that I live so long," for death will be overthrown, and health will be unfailing. At that time, there will be no more anxiety, only blessed joy and sweet and pleasant fellowship.

Oh, if only you could see the everlasting crowns of the saints in heaven and how much glory they now enjoy—those same saints who, when they were alive, were held in utter contempt by the world and were thought unworthy of even drawing breath. Doubtless you would at once humble yourself to the very dust and would seek rather to be everyone's servant than anyone's master. You would not long for the joyful days of this life, but would rather rejoice in bearing any hardship for God's sake and count it the greatest gain to be thought of as a humble servant to all.

Oh, if you found relish in these thoughts and allowed them to penetrate deep into your heart, how would you dare to complain even once! Are not all painful labors to be endured for eternal life? It is no small thing to lose or gain the kingdom of God! So, lift your face to heaven. Look at me and all my saints with me, they who in this world have had great contention. They are now joyful, they are now consoled, they are now safe, they are now at rest, and they will forever remain with me in my Father's kingdom.

Chapter 48

f Life and of Eternity

Disciple:

O most blessed mansion of the supreme city! O most bright day of eternity, which is never hidden by night but is always shot through with the light of the highest truth! O day always happy, always secure and never changing into night! Oh, that this day would dawn and all these passing things would come to an end! That day, indeed, shines upon the saints with resplendent and everlasting brightness. But to us who are still on our earthly pilgrimage, it is seen only from afar and as through a glass, darkly. The citizens of heaven know how joyful that day is, but

we poor banished children of Eve mourn that this day is bitter and wearisome.

The days of this life are short and evil, full of sorrow and misery,
where a person is stained with many sins, ensnared by many passions,
bound by many fears, swollen by many cares, distracted by many curi-
osities, entangled by many vanities, surrounded by many mistakes,
weakened by many efforts, weighed down by temptations, sapped by
pleasures, tormented by want.

Oh, when will there be an end to all these things that have gone awry
in God's plan? When shall I be freed from the wretched slavery of my
sins? When shall I be mindful, Lord, of you alone? When shall I fully
rejoice in you? When shall I be truly free, without anything standing in
my way, with no inner confusion and conflict? When shall I find a solid
peace—peace calm and secure, peace inside and out, peace firm in
every way? O good Jesus, when shall I see you face to face? When shall
I contemplate the glory of your kingdom? When will you be all in all to
me? Oh, when shall I be with you in your kingdom, which you have
prepared for your beloved from all eternity?

I am left poor and adrift in a hostile land where each day there are
wars and great misfortunes. Console me in my exile. Relieve me in my
sorrow, for my every desire longs after you. All that this world offers
me for comfort is a burden. I long to embrace you in the very depths of
my being, but I cannot take hold of you. I wish to cling to heavenly
things, but the things of this world and my undisciplined passions drag
me down. In my mind I wish to rise above all things, but against my will
I subject myself to them. So, unhappy person that I am, I struggle with
myself and become a burden to myself, because the spirit soars upward
but the rest of me gravitates downward.

Oh, how I suffer inside! While my mind thinks of heavenly things, a
disorderly mob of carnal thoughts confronts my prayers. O my God, do
not be far from me. In your wrath, do not turn away from your servant.
Flash your lightening and you will scatter them; shoot your arrows and
confound all these phantoms of the enemy. Call my thoughts back to
you. Make me forget everything that is not you. Help me to fling away
the evil phantoms. Help me to despise them. Come to my aid, eternal

Truth, so that no vanity may entice me. Come, heavenly sweetness, and let every impurity flee before your face.

Pardon me, too, and mercifully forgive me for the times that I think of things other than you during my prayers. Truly, I confess that I have been in the habit of allowing my mind to wander. Many times my mind is not where my body is, but it is where my thoughts have carried me. I am there where my thoughts are, and my thoughts are usually there with the things I care about the most. That thing which most quickly enters my thoughts is that which naturally pleases me or that which has become pleasing to me through habit; whence you, the Truth, have clearly said: "Where your treasure is, there also will be your heart."

If I love heaven, I gladly think of heavenly things. If I love the world instead of you, I put you out of my mind and rejoice in the world's happiness and become sad in its troubles. If I love the body, my imagination often dwells on it. If I love the spirit, I delight to think of spiritual things. Whatever it is that I love, I eagerly talk about and hear about, and I bring mental images of it home to myself.

But blessed is that person, Lord, who looks to you alone, who struggles against his twisted nature, and through intense spiritual desire nails to the tree all of the uncontrolled thoughts and desires that run through his mind. Then, with a serene conscience he may offer you unspotted prayer. Then, having shut himself off from all distractions, both inside and out, he may become worthy to be counted among the angelic choir.

Chapter 49

f Longing for Eternal Life and of the Promise It Holds

Jesus:

Dear friend, when you feel the desire for eternal happiness poured into you from above and when you long to leave your body behind in order to gaze upon my unchanging and never-shadowed brightness, open your heart wide and receive this holy inspiration with deep longing. Offer the greatest thanks to the divine goodness which deals so graciously with you, which visits you with mercy, which encourages you so warmly, and which powerfully lifts you up. Without it, your own weight will drag you down, for it is not by your own thought or effort that you receive this gift, but only by the favor of heaven's grace and of God's love for you. You receive it so that you may grow in virtue and humility, so that you may ready yourself for the coming struggles, and so that you may cling to me with all your heart and serve me with a burning desire.

My friend, the fire often burns, but the flame does not ascend without smoke. So, too, some people have a burning desire for heavenly things, but they are not yet free from feelings rooted deeply in the dark recesses of their own hearts. Thus, what they so earnestly ask of God, they ask not solely to honor him but to satisfy themselves, as well. This is frequently the case with you, too, though you may insist that it is not. Nothing is pure and perfect which is tainted by self-interest. Do not ask what is pleasing and of benefit to you but what is acceptable to me and what honors me. If you view things properly, you ought to prefer following my desires rather than your own.

I know what you want, and I have heard your frequent sighs. You wish to share in the glorious freedom of God's children now. You would be delighted to be already in the eternal home and heavenly country, filled with joy. But that hour has not yet come, for there is still another time, a time of struggle, a time of toil and testing.

You wish to be filled with the supreme good, but you cannot attain to it right now. I am that supreme good. Wait for me, says the Lord, until the kingdom of God comes. You still have to be tested and tried out in many things. Comfort will sometimes be given to you, but not fully. Take courage, then, and be strong in doing and enduring the things that go against your natural feelings. You must become a new person, changed into someone else. You must often do what you do not want to do, and what you want to do you must sometimes set aside. What pleases others will succeed; what pleases you will not. What others say will be heard; what you say will not. Others will ask and receive; you will ask and receive nothing. Others will be praised; you will be ignored. Others will be entrusted with this or that responsibility; you will be thought useless.

Sometimes all this will naturally upset you, but it will be to your great advantage if you put up with it in silence. In these and in many similar things the faithful servant of the Lord is tried. Often the most difficult trials involve enduring things that go against your will, especially when what you are asked to do seems stupid and pointless. And since, as a monk, you are under obedience and must not resist a higher authority, it seems hard to you to walk at another's beck and call and to forget your own ideas. But think of the fruit of your labors, of how quickly they will end, and of the great reward that will accompany them. Then you will have no complaints; then you will have only the strongest comfort for your patience.

In trade for that small measure of will that you freely give up now, things will always go your way in heaven. There you shall find all that you wish, all that you can desire. There you will enjoy having every good without the fear of losing it. There your will, at one with mine, will never desire anything extraneous or anything that is not me. There no one will work against you or complain about you, no one will get in your way, nothing will block your path. Instead, every good that you desire will be before you at the same time, all replenishing your love, all filled to overflowing. There I shall give you glory for the insults you have suffered, a robe of praise for your sorrow, a royal seat forever for your present humble position. There the fruit of obedience will be made known. There the work of penance will be turned to joy. And there humble obedience will be gloriously crowned.

Since this is the case, bow yourself humbly under the hands of all. Do not care who said what or who is ordering you about. Pay most attention to this: Whether a superior, a junior, or an equal asks anything of you, take it all in good stride and do your best to do as he wishes. Let one seek this and another that. Let one seek glory in this and another in that and be praised thousands upon thousands of times. As for you, have none of it. Rejoice only in deep humility and in pleasing and honoring only me. Let this be your wish: whether through life or through death, that God may always be glorified in you.

Chapter 50

ow a Lonely Person Should Place Himself in God's Hands

Disciple:

Lord God, holy Father, may you be blessed both now and forever, for as you will things to be, so they are, and what you do is always good. Let your servant find joy in you and not in himself or in anyone else, for you alone are true joy. You are my hope and my reward. You are my joy and my honor, O Lord. What does your servant have except what he has received from you—and without deserving it on his part? What you have given and what you have made are all yours. I am poor and have struggled amidst hardship since my youth, and my soul is saddened at times even to the point of tears whenever it is troubled by passions bent on enveloping her.

I long for the joy of peace. I beg for the peace of your children whom you nurture by the light of your comfort. If you give peace, if you flood me with holy joy, the soul of your servant will be filled with music and will be devout in your praise. But if you take yourself away, as you often do, he will not be able to follow your commandments. Instead, he will fall on his knees and strike his breast, because today is not like yesterday when your lamp shone over his head, and in the shadow of your wings he was protected from temptation's assault.

O just and ever-praiseworthy Father, the hour has come for your servant to be tested. Beloved Father, it is fitting that at this hour your servant should suffer something for you. O Father, ever-worshipped, the hour has come, which from all eternity you knew would arrive, when for a short time your servant would break down and be overwhelmed, though in his heart he would be with you through it all. For a little while he will be ridiculed, humiliated and brought to nothing in the eyes of other people; he will be crushed with sufferings and weariness. All this will happen so that he may arise with you again in the dawn of a new day and be glorified in heaven.

O holy Father, you have declared it to be so. Such is your will. And since you have ordained it this way, it has come to pass. This is a grace to your friend that he should suffer and be afflicted in this world for love of you, no matter how often, by what means or from what person it comes. Nothing on earth happens without your allowing it to happen and without your knowing about it beforehand.

It is good for me, Lord, that you have humbled me so that I may learn how you think and so that I may toss aside all pride and presumption. It is for my own good that shame has covered my face, that I may look to you for comfort rather than to others. I have learned also from this to hold in reverence your mysterious judgments which affect both the good with the bad, but not without equity and justice. I thank you for having not overlooked my failings but for having worn me down with blows of anguish and distress, for inflicting sorrows and limitations from without and within. Of all things under heaven there is none that can comfort me but you, Lord, my God, heavenly physician of souls, you who wound and heal, who drag down to the depths and lead back up again.

Your discipline is upon me and your rod itself shall teach me. See, beloved Father, I am in your hands. I bend myself under your correcting rod. Strike my back and my neck that I may bend my crooked ways to your will. Make me a holy and humble disciple as you have so kindly done for others, so that I may always walk according to your least desire. I entrust myself and all that is mine to your correction. It is better to be rebuked here than in the life to come.

You know each and every thing; nothing in our consciences lies hidden from you. You know the future before it happens, and you do not need us to remind you of what is happening on earth. You know what I need for my spiritual progress. You know how much tribulation helps to scour away the rust of sin. Do with me as you wish, and do not turn your back on my sinful life. You know me better and more clearly than anyone else. Grant me, Lord, to know what I ought to know, to love what I ought to love, to praise what is most pleasing to you, to esteem what seems most precious to you, to detest what is loathsome in your eyes. Let me not judge according to outward appearances nor condemn according to what people hear, but with true judgment let me discern between material and spiritual matters, and above all let me always seek to know your will.

Our senses often mislead our judgments, and those who love only this world are likewise deceived in loving only the things they see. Is a person any better because others think him so? A deceitful person deceives the deceiver, the vain person the vain, the blind person the blind, the weak person the weak. Truly, the more such people flatter each other, the more they deceive each other. As the humble Saint Francis says, "A person is only as great as he is in your eyes—and no more."

Chapter 51

hat We Must Perform Humble Works When We Are Unable to Perform Higher Ones

Jesus:

My dear friend, your desire for virtue cannot always remain at a fever pitch nor will you always hold steady in a lofty flight of contemplation. Because of original sin's corruption, you will sometimes descend to lesser things and bear the burden of a decaying life, even though it will be against your will and may weary you. As long as you wander about the world in this mortal body you will know weariness and a heavy heart. Therefore, while you are in the flesh you ought often to bemoan the burden of it, for because of it you cannot fully devote yourself to the spiritual life and to divine contemplation.

When this happens, it is good for you to take refuge in humble, outward tasks and to refresh yourself in good works. Await my coming and my heavenly visit with calm assurance and patiently bear your exile and mental dryness until I come to you and free you from all your worries. I shall cause you to forget your troubles and to enjoy inner peace. I shall spread open before you the pleasant fields of Holy Scripture, so that with open heart you may begin to run in the way of my commandments. And then you will say: "the sufferings of this present time are not worthy to be compared with the future glory that is to be revealed in us."

Chapter 52

hat We Should Not Think Ourselves Worthy of Comfort but Deserving of Correction

Disciple:

Lord, I am not worthy of your comfort nor am I worthy of your company. When you leave me poor and desolate you only treat me as I deserve. Even if I were to shed a sea of tears I would still be unworthy of your consolation. I deserve nothing but to be scourged and punished, for I have often gravely offended you, and in many things I have fallen far short of what you expect. Therefore, according to right reason, I do not deserve even the least of your consolations.

But you, O clement and merciful God, do not want to see your works perish. And in order to show the riches of your goodness toward the vessels of your mercy, you stoop to console your servant. Such comfort is immeasurable and is beyond anything I deserve. Your consolation is so unlike even the most pleasant human conversation! What have I done, Lord, that you should console me from heaven? I recall nothing good that I have done, but I do recall always running headlong into vice and being reluctant to change my ways. It is true, and I cannot deny it. If I were to say otherwise, you would give me the lie and no one would stand up for me. What have I deserved for my sins but hell and eternal fire? In truth, I admit that I deserve all scorn and contempt, and I am not fit to be counted among those who are devoted to you. And though I hear this reluctantly, yet, for truth's sake, I admit my sins so that I may more readily deserve to beg your mercy.

What shall I say, guilty and full of confusion as I am? My mouth can utter nothing but this: "I have sinned, O Lord, I have sinned. Have mercy on me and pardon me." Give me a short time that I may mourn my sorrow before I go to a land that is dark and blanketed with the mist of death. What do you most require of a guilty and wretched sinner but that he should be disgusted with himself and humble himself for his failures? In true contrition and humility of heart is born the hope of forgiveness; the troubled conscience is reconciled; lost grace is recovered; we are saved from future wrath; and God and the repentant soul meet in a holy embrace.

Humble sorrow for sins is an acceptable offering to you, Lord, far sweeter in your sight than the fragrance of burning incense. This is also the pleasing ointment which you wished to be poured on your holy feet, for you have never turned your back on a contrite and humble heart. The place of refuge from the enemy's angry face is here. At your feet whatever dirt one has picked up along life's journey is washed away.

Chapter 53

hat God's Grace Does Not Mix with the Wisdom of the World

Jesus:

My dear friend, my grace is precious. It does not allow itself to mix with anything else. You must, therefore, cast aside everything that stands in the way of grace if you wish it to pour over you. Seek a quiet place for yourself, and love to linger there alone. Do not look for idle chit-chat, but pour forth devout prayers to God that you may keep your mind focused on feeling deep sorrow for those times you have failed him and on maintaining a clear conscience. Look upon the whole world as nothing without God, and prefer serving God to anything else. You cannot serve me and amuse yourself in passing fancies, too. Seek times for privacy even from friends and loved ones, and do not dwell on the comforts of this world. For this reason the blessed apostle Peter instructed the faithful followers of Christ to keep themselves as strangers and pilgrims in this world.

Oh, what confidence will that person have at death who is not held back by attachments to anything in the world! But a weak person cannot bear to have his heart cut loose from everything nor can one who clings to the world understand the freedom of one who does not. Yet, if a person truly wishes to have a spiritual life, he must place God first. And having placed God first, he must look to God's love as the most important thing in life. If you keep God at the center of your life, you will easily overcome all other things. The perfect victory is to be at one with God; the person who is, is master of himself and lord of the world.

If you wish to climb to this height, you must begin bravely and lay the axe to the root; pull up and destroy every movement toward self-centered, selfish desires. All that must be radically overcome is rooted in this vice of making yourself the center of your own world. When this evil is mastered and brought under control, great peace and calm will follow. But because few people strive to rise above themselves in such a way, they remain entangled in a fibery web and their spirits can never soar on high. Whoever wishes to walk freely with me must put an end to all excessive attachments and cling to no person or created thing out of a grasping self-love.

Chapter 54

f the Differing Movements of Nature and Grace

Jesus:

My friend, pay particular attention to the movements of nature and grace, for they move in opposite ways and with such great subtlety that they can hardly be distinguished except by a spiritual and inwardly enlightened person. Certainly, everyone desires what is good, and everyone claims that there is something good in everything they say and do. Thus, many people are tricked by what seems to be good.

Nature is crafty and seduces many. It entangles them and deceives them, and it is always self-centered in the end. But grace walks in simplicity and turns away from all forms of evil. It offers no deceit and does everything purely for God, in whom it rests as its final goal.

Nature is unwilling to be mortified, to be held in check, to be overcome, to be less than others or to be under a yoke of obedience. But grace focuses on growing beyond self-centeredness, resisting sensuality, wanting to be submissive, desiring to be overcome, not exercising its own freedom, loving to be disciplined, and not wishing to dominate anyone. It wants to live, to stay, and to be under God. For God's sake, grace is always willing to submit itself humbly to everyone.

Nature works for its own benefit and keeps an eye out for what it can gain from someone else. Grace, on the other hand, does not consider what is useful and advantageous to itself but what is beneficial to many. Nature willingly accepts honor and respect, but grace faithfully attributes all honor and glory to God. Nature is afraid of shame and contempt, but grace is happy to suffer reproach for the name of Jesus. Nature is lazy, but grace joyfully looks for something productive to do. Nature seeks to have curious and beautiful things and dislikes things common and rude, but grace delights in simple and humble things, does not reject those that are rough hewn, and does not refuse to wear old, shabby clothes.

Nature keeps an eye on fashion, it rejoices at material gain, it is depressed at loss, and it is irritated at every word that it even suspects might be an affront. But grace attends to eternal things and does not cling to passing ones, neither is it upset at the loss of material things nor is it provoked by every harsh word, for it places its joy and treasure in heaven where nothing perishes.

Nature is greedy and likes to take rather than to give, and it loves personal and private things. Grace, on the other hand, is kind and sharing, shuns selfishness, is content with little, and considers it more blessed to give than to receive.

Nature inclines a person to created things, to his own body, to vanities, and to scurrying about being busy. But grace draws one to God and to virtue, turns its back on anything that stands between it and God, does not get caught up in worldly affairs at the expense of spiritual ones, travels little, and blushes to appear in public.

Nature gladly accepts any outside comfort that may gratify the senses, but grace seeks comfort in God alone and delights in the supreme good rather than in anything that is seen.

Nature does everything for its own gain and interest. It can do nothing without pay. In exchange for a kindness, it hopes for something equal or better in return—or else it demands praise or a favor—for it is eager to have its deeds and gifts be recognized by everyone. Grace seeks nothing temporal, though. It asks for no reward other than God alone, and it wants nothing more of this life than the necessities that may help it to gain eternal life.

Nature revels in many friends and relatives, glories in noble estates and impressive genealogies, smiles on those in power, flatters the wealthy, and applauds those who look and behave like itself. Grace, however, loves even its enemies, is not puffed up over a crowd of friends, and does not put much stock in rank or birth, unless it suggests greater virtue. Grace favors the poor to the rich, has more feeling for the innocent than the powerful, rejoices with the honest and not the false, and always encourages the good to desire better gifts and to become more like the Son of God by exercising virtue.

Nature is quick to complain of want and of trouble. Grace bears poverty resolutely. Nature turns all things to itself, pushes itself into the spotlight, and fights to keep itself there. Grace, though, refers all things to God, from whom they have all come. Grace ascribes no good to itself, nor does it arrogantly push itself forward. It does not argue or prefer its own opinion to others. In every feeling and understanding grace submits itself to eternal wisdom and divine scrutiny.

Nature longs to know secrets and to have the inside story on the latest news. It wishes to be seen in public and to be steeped in sensual experience. Nature wants to be noticed by others and to do those things that bring praise and admiration. But grace does not care to hear novel things or to latch on to curious ideas, for all this springs from the old corruption. After all, nothing is new or lasting upon this earth. Grace teaches us, therefore, to restrain the senses, to avoid empty satisfaction and hollow display, and humbly to hide those things that are worthy of praise and admiration. Grace teaches us to seek what is useful to the soul and to quest after the praise and honor of God. Everything it has done and everything it has learned is directed to this end. Grace does not wish itself or what it has done to be praised, but wishes that God, who lavishes all things out of pure love, should be blessed in his gifts.

Grace is a supernatural light and a special gift of God, the distinguishing mark of his chosen ones. It is an assurance of eternal salvation. It raises a person from earthly things to the love of heavenly things, and it transforms him from a conceited, self-centered person into a spiritual one. The more nature is curbed and subdued, the more grace is poured in, and by the Lord coming to him anew each day, a person is refashioned after the image of God, deep within his soul.

Chapter 55

Of Fallen Nature and of the Effect of Divine Grace

Disciple:

O Lord, my God, you have created me in your own image and likeness. Grant me this grace which you have shown to be of such great importance for salvation: that I may overcome my flawed nature that draws me to sin and ruin. In my body I feel the law of sin working against the law of my mind, leading me captive to obey fallen nature in many things. I cannot resist its urgings unless I am helped by your holy grace, ardently poured into my heart.

I need your grace—and I need it in great quantities—to overcome nature, which has been prone to evil from the beginning. Ever since nature fell and became infected by the sin of Adam, the first man, the punishments of that offense have fallen on all mankind. Nature itself, which you made good and without flaw, now represents vice and weakness; its natural tendency, if left to itself, drags everything down.

The little strength that remains is but the faint glow of an ember hidden beneath the ashes. It is natural reason itself, shrouded in great darkness, still having the ability to judge between good and evil, true and false. But it is not able to act on all that it knows to be right nor does it possess the full light of truth any longer or the absolute purity of its affections.

So it is, my God, that in the depths of my soul I delight in your law and know that your commands are good, just and holy, for they encourage us to flee from all evil and sin. And yet, as I am, I serve the law of sin, and all the while I obey sensuality rather than reason. Hence, it is within my power to want that which is good, but I cannot find the strength to achieve it. Hence, too, I often make many good plans, but because I lack grace to help my weakness, I pull back and hesitate at the slightest resistance. So it happens that I know the way of perfection and see clearly enough what I ought to do, but crushed under the weight of my own corruption, I do not pick myself up and press on to better things.

Oh, how absolutely necessary is your grace for me, Lord, if I am to begin anything good, to continue on with it, and to see it through to the end. Without it, I can do nothing; with it strengthening me, I can do everything. O true heavenly grace, without which our merits are nothing and our natural abilities are worthless! No arts, no wealth, no beauty or strength, no wit or eloquence are of any value in your eyes, Lord, without grace.

The good and the bad share nature's gifts, but grace is the special gift of God's chosen ones. Being sealed with it, they are counted worthy of eternal life. This grace is so excellent that neither the gift of prophesy nor the working of miracles nor any flight of divine imagination is worth anything without it. Indeed, neither faith nor hope nor any of the other virtues is acceptable to you without grace and love.

Oh, most blessed grace! You make the poor in spirit rich in virtues, and you make those who are blessed with many good things humble of heart. Come, descend upon me. Fill me early in the morning with your comfort so that my soul does not faint through weariness and dryness. O Lord, I pray that I may find favor in your eyes. Your grace is enough for me even if I receive none of those things which nature desires. When I am tempted and afflicted with many troubles, I shall fear no evil as long as your grace is with me. It is my strength. It brings me comfort and help. It is stronger than all my enemies and wiser than all the wise. Your grace is the mistress of truth, teacher of discipline, light of the heart, comforter of the anguished. It banishes sorrow, chases away fears, nurses devotion, and brings tears to the eyes. Without your grace what am I but dried out tinder, a useless stump, fit only to be cast aside? Therefore, Lord, let your grace always go before me and follow me and make me ever intent upon good works, through Jesus Christ, your Son. Amen.

Chapter 56

**hat We Should Turn from Ourselves
and Imitate Christ by Way of the Cross**

Jesus:

My dear friend, the more you can leave yourself behind, the more you will be able to enter into me. Just as longing for nothing outside of yourself makes for inner peace, so does letting go of yourself unite you with God. I want you to learn to abandon yourself perfectly to my will, without grumbling or complaining.

Follow me. I am the Way, the Truth, and the Life. Without the Way, there is no going; without the Truth, there is no knowing; without the Life, there is no living. I am the Way you are to follow. I am the Truth you are to believe. I am the Life you are to hope for. I am the Way that cannot be destroyed, the Truth that cannot be wrong, the Life that cannot be ended. I am the Way that is most straight, the supreme Truth, the true Life, the blessed Life, begotten, not made.

If you continue in my way you will know the truth, and the truth will set you free. You will have eternal life. If you wish to enter into life, keep the commandments. If you wish to know the truth, believe in me. If you wish to be perfect, sell all that you have. If you wish to be my follower, deny your very self. If you wish to have a blessed life, see this present life for what it is. If you wish to be exalted in heaven, humble yourself in this world. If you wish to reign with me, carry my cross, for only the servants of the cross find the road of blessedness and true light.

Disciple:

Lord Jesus, since your life was lived within narrow confines, and since it was scorned by the world, grant that I may imitate you by bearing whatever burdens you choose to send me, for the servant is not greater than his lord nor is the student greater than his teacher. Let your servant be trained by the example of your life, for there will I find my salvation and true holiness. Whatever I read or hear apart from that neither refreshes nor delights me.

Jesus:

My dear friend, since you know these things and have read all about them, blessed will you be if you do them. Anyone who hears my commands—and keeps them—shall see me and shall sit with me in my Father's kingdom.

Disciple:

Lord Jesus, let it be as you have said and promised. Oh, that I may deserve it! I have shouldered the weight of your cross. I have taken it from your hands. You have placed it upon me, and I shall bear it, yes, even unto death. Truly, the life of a good monk—or of any good Christian—is a cross, but it is also his compass to paradise. Now that we have begun the journey, we must not go backward or give up.

So, come along! Let us go forward together! Jesus will be with us. For Jesus's sake we took up this cross; for Jesus's sake let us stick with it. Our Commander will be our helper. He has already scouted out the road. Look! our King marches ahead of us and will fight for us! Let us follow him courageously; let no one shrink at the terror! Let us be ready to die bravely in battle! Let us not stain our glory by deserting the cross!

Chapter 57

hat We Should Not Be Too Dejected When We Fail

Jesus:

My dear friend, patience and humility in troubled times are more pleasing to me than much comfort and devotion in prosperous ones. Why do you let little things said against you upset you so? Even if more had been said you should not have been disturbed. But let it go for now. It is nothing new. This is not the first time that it has happened, and if you live a long life, it will not be the last.

You are brave as long as no misfortune comes your way. You can give good advice, and you know how to strengthen others with your words. But when any calamity suddenly knocks at your door, your counsel and courage duck out the back way! Remember your great weakness which you have often experienced in small difficulties. Yet, these small difficulties—and others like them—were meant for your salvation each time they happened.

Put each trouble out of your heart as best you can. If it has touched you, do not let it knock you down or keep you caught in its web for long. If you cannot suffer it joyfully, at least suffer it patiently. And even if you would rather not hear such remarks, and feel irritated when you do, hold your tongue. Let no rash word slip from your mouth that may shock or disillusion those little ones who are new to the spiritual life. Your excitement will soon settle down and the return of grace will turn your inner sorrow into something sweet.

I am still ready to help you and comfort you even more than before, if you trust in me and call upon me in a prayerful way. Take courage and get set for even greater demands on your endurance. If you feel yourself often set upon or badly tempted, still all is not lost. You are not God; you are a human being. You are flesh; you are not an angel. How can you always carry on in unwavering virtue when Lucifer could not while he was in heaven nor could Adam while he was in paradise? I am the one who raises to safety those who mourn, and I am the one who invites you to share in my divinity. But I only advance those who recognize their own weakness.

Disciple:

Lord, blessed be your word, sweeter to my mouth than honey and the honeycomb. What would I do in my trials and tribulations if you did not strengthen me with your holy words? What does it matter how many trials I endure or what kind they may be as long as I come to a safe harbor in the end? Grant me a good end. Grant me a happy passage from this world. Remember me, my God, and lead me along the right path to your kingdom. Amen.

Chapter 58

Of Not Prying into Things That Are beyond Our Understanding

Jesus:

Dear friend, be wary of discussing lofty topics and God's hidden judgments. Do not ask why one person is so forsaken while another is raised up to such a grace, or why one person is so badly afflicted while another is highly exalted. These things are beyond our understanding, and no amount of reasoning or discussion can penetrate into the judgments of God. So, when the enemy suggests such things to you or curious people ask you about them, answer with the Prophet: "You are just, Lord, and your judgment is right." Or like this: "The judgments of the Lord are true, justified in themselves." My judgments are to be respected, not debated, for they are incomprehensible to human understanding.

In the same way, do not pry into or argue about the merits of the saints. Do not bicker over who is more holy or who is greater in the kingdom of heaven. Such questions often breed strife and useless contention, they nourish pride and presumption, and all this gives rise to envy and dissension, as one puts forward his saint and another proudly prefers his own.

To wish to know such things and to pry into them does no one any good; instead, it greatly displeases the saints. I am not the God of strife but of peace, and this peace consists more in true humility than in patronage. Some people are drawn to one saint or another as suits their personal feelings, but these feelings come more from them than from me.

I am the one who made all the saints. I gave them grace. I am responsible for their glory. I know the merits of each. I went out and awaited each one with many blessings. I knew who my beloved ones would be before the beginning of time. I chose them from out of the world; they did not choose me. I called them by grace and attracted them by mercy. I led them safely through many temptations. I drenched them in lavish consolations. I gave them perseverance. I have crowned their patience. I know who is first and who is last. I embrace them all with a boundless love. I am to be praised in my saints, and above all I am to be blessed and honored in each one of them whom I have so gloriously magnified and chosen without any regard for any merits on their part.

Therefore, the person who looks down on one of the least of my saints shows no honor for the greatest, for I made both the small and the great, and anyone who detracts from even one of the saints detracts also from me and from all the others in the kingdom of heaven. They are all one through the bond of love: They all think the same thoughts; they all have the same desires; and they all love one another. But what is even more wonderful than this is that they all love me more than themselves and their own worth, for having been raised far above themselves, and having been drawn away from self-love, they are completely absorbed in their love of me. In me they rest and become complete. There is nothing that can turn them away from me or discourage them, for they are full of eternal Truth and they burn with the fire of divine love which will never go out.

Therefore, let those people who are caught up in the day-to-day business of asserting themselves, those people who love nothing but themselves and their own point of view, keep quiet about the status of the saints. They add and subtract from their glory as it suits their fancy and not as it pleases eternal Truth.

Many people behave this way out of pure ignorance. This is especially true of those spiritual dimwits who do not know how to love anyone as they should. They are drawn to one saint because his or her life is appealing, or to another saint because a friend likes him! They imagine that since that is the way things work on earth, they must work that way in heaven, too! There is an enormous gap between the thoughts of such a person and the thoughts of one who sees through eyes made clear by a heavenly light.

So be careful, my friend, of becoming too curious about things which outpace your understanding. Instead, aim at this: that you may be found in the kingdom of God even if you are the least important person there. And if anyone were to know which saint is the holier in the kingdom of heaven or which one is the greater, what good would this knowledge do him, unless knowing it, he would humble himself even more in my sight and give greater praise to my name?

That person is much more acceptable to God who thinks of the greatness of his own sins, of how little he has progressed in virtue, and of how far away he is from the perfection of the saints, than is the person who argues about who is the greater or lesser among them. It is better to call upon the saints with devout prayers and tears and with a humble mind to ask for their help than it is to nag them with silly questions. The saints are perfectly and completely content. Now, if only people would learn how to stop wagging their tongues!

The saints do not pride themselves on their own merits, for they ascribe nothing good to themselves but all to me, because I gave them everything out of my infinite love. They are filled with so great a love for God and they have such an overflowing joy, that for them their glory lacks nothing, their happiness lacks nothing. It is this way with all the saints: The higher they are in glory, the more humble they are in themselves, the closer they are to me, and the more they are beloved by me. Thus, you have it written: "They cast down their crowns before God and fell on their faces before the Lamb, and they adored him who lives forever and ever."

Many seek to discover who is the greatest in the kingdom of God without knowing if they themselves will be worthy to be numbered among the least. It is a great thing to be even the least in heaven where all are great, because all will be called and all will be children of God. The least will be priceless, and the sinner, though he may be a hundred years old, will die. When the disciples asked who was the greatest in the kingdom of heaven, they heard this reply: "Unless you turn yourselves around and become like little children, you will never enter the kingdom of heaven." Therefore, whoever humbles himself like a child is the greatest in the kingdom of heaven.

Woe to those who think themselves too good to humble themselves willingly with the children, for the lowly gate of the heavenly kingdom will not allow them to enter. Woe also to the rich who have their comforts here, for while the poor shall enter into the kingdom of God, they will stand outside lamenting. Rejoice, you humble! Exult, you poor! The kingdom of God is yours if you walk in the way of truth!

Chapter 59

hat All Hope and Trust Should Be Fixed on God Alone

Disciple:

Lord, what can I rely on in this life? What is my greatest comfort among all the things that appear under heaven? Is it not you, my Lord God, whose mercies are without number? When did things ever go well with me without you? When did things ever go badly with you at my side? I would rather be poor for your sake than rich without you. I would rather be a pilgrim wandering the earth with you than be in heaven without you. Where you are, there is heaven; where you are not, there is death and hell. You are everything I long for. Thus, I must sigh for you, cry out after you and prevail upon you. There is no one in whom I can fully confide for help in times of need except you alone, my God. You are my hope, my assurance, my comforter. You are faithful in all things.

Everyone looks out for himself. Only you look out for my salvation and progress and see to it that all things work to my good. Even if you expose me to temptations and hardships, you, who are given to testing your loved ones in a thousand ways, shape it all to my benefit. In testing me this way you should be loved and praised no less than if you had filled me with heavenly consolations. So in you, Lord God, I place all my hope and seek all my shelter. Before you I place all my troubles and anxieties. Everything that is not you I find frail and unstable. Having many friends will be of no help to me nor can powerful associates aid me. Prudent advisors cannot help me nor can learned books comfort me. Wealth cannot ransom me nor can any hidden place keep me safe. None of this will help if you yourself do not aid, comfort, console, teach and care for me. All things that seem to be for our peace and happiness are nothing without you. Truly, they bring us no happiness at all.

You are the object of all good, the apex of life, the depth of wisdom. Your servants' greatest consolation is to hope in you above all things. I turn my eyes to you. In you, my God, Father of mercies, I place my trust. Bless my soul and make it holy with your heavenly blessing; let it become your holy dwelling, the place of your eternal glory. Let nothing be found in your temple that may offend the eyes of your majesty.

According to the greatness of your goodness and your many mercies, look down on me and hear the prayer of your poor servant, exiled far off in the land of the shadow of death. Protect and keep the soul of your servant, traveling amid the many dangers of life. By your grace, direct him along the path of peace until he is back home in the land of everlasting brightness. Amen.

BOOK 4

*The Book
on the Sacrament*

Chapter 1

ith What Great Reverence Christ Should be Received

The Voice of Christ

Come to me all you who labor and are burdened, and I shall refresh you. The bread that I shall give for the life of the world is my flesh. Take and eat; this is my body, which is given for you. Do this in memory of me. If you eat my flesh and drink my blood, you will abide in me and I in you. The words that I have spoken to you are spirit and life.

Disciple:

These are your words, Christ, the eternal Truth, though they were not said all at one time nor written all in one place. Therefore, since they are yours and they are true, I should receive them all with gratitude and certainty. They are your words and you have spoken them; they are also mine, for you have said them for my salvation. I accept them gladly from your lips that they may be the more deeply imprinted on my heart.

Words filled with such great tenderness, sweetness and love stir me, but my own sins frighten me and my muddied conscience holds me back from sharing in such great mysteries. Your sweet words call me to you, but my many offenses weigh me down. You command me to come to you with confidence if I wish to share your life and to receive the food of immortality, if I wish to gain eternal life and glory.

"Come to me," you say, "all you who labor and are burdened, and I shall refresh you." Oh, sweet and lovable words to the ear of one who constantly disappoints you, that you, O Lord, my God, invite the poor

164

and the needy to Communion in your most sacred Body. But who am I, Lord, that I should presume to come to you? The heaven of heavens cannot contain you and yet you say, "Come to me, all of you." What does this mean, this most loving deference and friendly invitation? How can I dare to come, I who know of not a single good thing that I have done to deserve your love? How can I bring you into the place where I live, I who have so often offended you in front of your own loving eyes? Angels and archangels stand before you in awe, the saints and all the good people who have ever lived hold you in great reverence, and still you say, "Come to me, all of you."

Except that you said this yourself, Lord, who would believe it to be true? And except that you commanded it, who would dare try to approach? Think of this: Noah, a just man, worked a hundred years at building the ark in order that he and a few others might be saved. How can I—in one hour—prepare myself to receive with reverence the Creator of the world? Moses, your great servant and special friend, built an ark of incorruptible wood, which he covered with the purest gold in order to put away the tablets of the Law for safekeeping. Shall I, then, a wholly unworthy person, dare to receive you so lightly, the maker of the Law and the giver of life? Solomon, the wisest of Israel's kings, spent seven years building a magnificent temple in praise of your name, and for eight days he celebrated the feast of its dedication and sacrificed a thousand peace offerings, and with resounding trumpets and much joy he solemnly brought the ark of the Covenant to the place prepared for it. And I, who know in my own heart how unworthy I am, how shall I bring you into my home? Why, I scarcely know how to spend a half-hour in devout prayer. If only I could spend even that half-hour as I should!

O my God, how much they tried to please you! Alas! how little it is that I do! How little time I spend in preparing myself for Communion. Rarely am I entirely at one with myself, and even more rarely am I wholly free of distractions. Yet, surely, when I am in your saving presence no improper thought should occupy me nor should my mind wander to other things. It is not an angel but the Lord of angels that I am about to welcome as my guest. There is a vast difference between the ark of the Covenant with its relics and your most pure Body with its unutterable virtues; there is a vast difference between the sacrifices of the Law, which prefigured future events, and the true sacrifice of your Body, which completes all the ancient sacrifices.

Why then do I not burn with greater love in your holy presence? Why do I not prepare myself with greater care to receive your sacred gifts when those ancient, holy patriarchs, prophets, kings, and princes—together with all their people—showed such great love and devotion in worshiping you? The devout King David danced before the ark of God with all his might, recalling the blessings granted to his ancestors in times past. He invented various kinds of instruments, he composed psalms, and he taught his people how to sing them joyously. Filled with the inspiration of the Holy Spirit, he himself often played on the harp, and he taught Israel to praise God with all their hearts and with one voice to bless and proclaim him each and every day.

If the devotion and praise of God shown then in the presence of the ark of the Covenant was so great, then how great now should be the reverence and devotion of myself and of all Christian people in the presence of the Sacrament, in receiving the most excellent Body of Christ? Many people scurry about to various places to visit the relics of the saints and are amazed to hear of their marvelous deeds, to gaze at their splendid shrines, and to kiss their sacred bones, wrapped in silk and gold. But look! you are present to me here on the altar, my God, Holy of Holies, Creator of human beings, and Lord of angels. Often curiosity and the desire to see new things lead people to make pilgrimages. They seldom change their lives as a result, though, especially if they run from place to place with no real change of heart.

But in the Sacrament of the altar you are fully present, my God, in the person of Jesus Christ, and each time that you are worthily and devoutly received we enjoy the abundant fruit of eternal salvation. We are certainly not drawn to this Sacrament lightly nor are we drawn out of curiosity or a desire to please our appetites; rather, firm faith, devout hope and sincere love draw us to you. O God, unseen Creator of the universe, how wonderfully you treat us; how sweetly and graciously you care for those whom you have chosen to be your own, those to whom you offer yourself in this Sacrament. This surpasses all understanding, and it is this in particular that draws the hearts of devout people to you and that causes the soft glow of their love to burst into flame. Your true, faithful ones—those who spend their whole lives trying to change their ways—often receive the great grace of devotion and the love of doing what is right from this most worthy Sacrament.

O admirable and hidden grace of this Sacrament, which only Christ's faithful ones know! Those who lack faith and those who are the slaves of sin cannot experience such grace. In this Sacrament spiritual grace is granted, the soul's lost strength is restored, and its beauty, often disfigured by sin, returns again. And sometimes this grace is so great that, through the fullness of the devotion offered to God, not only the mind, but the weakened body as well, feels an increase in strength.

Hence, we should feel great sorrow and regret because of our coolness and negligence toward the Body of Christ; we should feel great sadness and disappointment for not being drawn with greater love to receive our Lord, in whom rests all the hope and merit of salvation. He himself is our path to holiness, our way to salvation; it is he who comforts us on our journey and who is the eternal happiness of the saints. So it is most sad to see that many people have such little regard for this saving mystery, this mystery that delights heaven and keeps the entire world intact.

Oh, how blind and hard is the human heart that does not pay greater attention to such a splendid gift as the Body of Christ. By making Communion a daily habit some people grow indifferent toward it. If in the whole world this most holy Sacrament were celebrated in only one place and were consecrated by only one priest, how great do you think people's desire would be to go to that place and to that priest of God so that they could see the divine mysteries celebrated? But now there are many priests, and Christ is offered up in many places, so that God's grace and his love for us appear the greater the more widely Holy Communion is distributed throughout the world.

I thank you, good Jesus, eternal Shepherd, for choosing to nourish us with your precious Body and Blood and for inviting us by your own words to share in these mysteries, saying: "Come to me all you who labor and are burdened, and I shall refresh you."

Chapter 2

hat Great Goodness and Love God Shows to Us in This Sacrament

Disciple:

Trusting in your great goodness and mercy, Lord, I come as one sick to the Healer, as one hungry and thirsty to the Source of life, as a beggar to the King of heaven, as a servant to the Lord, as a created being to the Creator, as one forsaken to my compassionate Comforter. But why should you come to me? Who am I that you should give yourself to me? How does someone like me dare to appear before you? And how can you stoop to come to me?

You know me, and you know that I am nothing at all apart from you, so why should you grant me this favor? I confess my unworthiness, and I acknowledge your goodness; I praise your kindness, and I thank you for your great love. You do this because you want to do it, not because I deserve it. You do this in order that your goodness may be better known to me, that your love may be more fully engendered in me, and that humility may be more attractive to me. So, since this pleases you, and because you have ordered it to be so, your regard for me pleases me too. Grant that my unworthiness may not get in the way!

O sweet and kind Jesus, what reverence and gratitude I owe to you; what unending praise should be yours each time I receive your sacred Body. No one can adequately explain what such a profound gift means. But what thoughts should be in my mind as I approach my Lord in this intimate sharing? I have never been able to worship you as I should, yet I wish to receive you with great devotion! What can I do that is better or of greater worth to my soul than to humble myself fully before you and to praise your goodness that is infinitely above me?

I praise you, my God, and I exalt you forever, but I look down upon myself and prostrate myself before you in my profound unworthiness. You see, you are the Saint of saints, and I am the sorriest of sinners. You, you see, bend down to me, who am unworthy to look up to you. And look! you come to me; you want to be with me; and you invite me to your banquet! You wish to give me heavenly food and the bread of angels to eat—nothing else, indeed, than your very self, the living bread who came down from heaven and who gives life to the world!

See from what place such love comes, how excellent the honor that radiates from it! What great thanksgiving and praises are due to you for this gift of yourself! Oh, how healing and helpful was your plan to give us this Sacrament! How sweet and joyful the banquet in which you gave yourself as food! Oh, how wonderful is your work, Lord, how powerful your goodness, and how forthright your truth! You spoke and all things were made; you willed it to be, and this Sacrament was made, too. It is a thing of wonder and a thing worthy of our faith that goes far beyond human understanding that you, O Lord, my God—true God and true man—are fully present under the appearance of bread and wine and that you are eaten by those who receive you, without being consumed!

Lord of all things, who have need of nothing, you have chosen to live among us through this Sacrament. Keep my heart and my body unblemished so that with a happy and pure conscience I may often celebrate and receive your mysteries for my eternal salvation—your mysteries, which you have given to us and made holy for your honor, celebrated forever in memory of you. Rejoice, my soul, and give thanks to God for leaving to you in this valley of tears so noble a gift, so unique a comfort. As often as we celebrate this mystery anew and receive the Body of Christ, so often do we perform the work of our redemption, and so often do we share in all those things that Christ has earned. Christ's love never fades, and his immense graciousness is never exhausted.

Therefore, we should always prepare ourselves for this Sacrament with a mind that is alert and receptive, seriously pondering this great mystery of salvation. Whenever we celebrate or attend Mass it should be as great, as new and as joyful as if on that same day Christ had just descended into the Virgin's womb to become our brother, or as if he were hanging on the cross suffering and dying for our salvation.

Chapter 3

 ow It Is Helpful to Receive Communion Often

Disciple:

Look, Lord! I come to you so that your gift may help me and so that I may delight in your holy banquet, which you, O God, in your sweetness have prepared for us. You see, you are all that I can or should desire; you are my salvation and redemption, my hope and my strength, my honor and my glory. Therefore, give joy to the soul of your servant this day, for to you, Lord Jesus, I lift up my soul.

Now I wish to receive you with devotion and reverence; I long to bring you into my house, so that like Zacchaeus, I may be worthy of your blessing and may be numbered among the children of Abraham. My soul deeply yearns for your Body; my heart longs to be one with you. Give yourself to me and that will be enough, for no comfort satisfies me apart from you. I cannot live without you; without you, I am unable to exist. Therefore, I must come to you often and receive you as the medicine of my salvation, lest, deprived of this heavenly food, I should faint in my journey through life. In just this way, most merciful Jesus, while you were preaching to the people and healing various diseases, you once said: "I am unwilling to send them home with nothing to eat, lest they faint on the way." Treat me as you treated them, you who have left yourself in this Sacrament for the comfort of your faithful ones, for you are the sweet refreshment of the soul, and whoever shall partake of you worthily shall inherit and share in eternal glory.

It is most necessary for me, who waver and sin so often and who so quickly become lazy and falter, that by frequent prayers and confessions and by receiving your holy Body, I may renew, purify, and enkindle myself. If I stay away from you too long, I may fall away from my holy resolve. Because we are so attracted to the values of this world, we continually drift away from you, and unless divine medicine is brought to us quickly, we soon find ourselves lost and alone. Holy Communion draws us back to you and comforts us in your goodness.

If I am so often careless and lukewarm when I go to Holy Communion or celebrate Mass, what would happen if I did not receive this medicine or seek your help? Though I may not be in the proper frame of mind to celebrate or attend Mass daily, still I should try to receive the divine mysteries at suitable times and make myself a participant in so great a grace. The faithful soul's chief comfort, while far away from you and traveling through life, is remembering God often and receiving the Lord with great devotion.

Oh, the marvelous goodness and kindness that you show to us that you, Lord God, Creator and giver of life, lower yourself to come to such a poor soul, and with the fullness of your divinity and humanity satisfy her hunger! O happy mind and blessed soul that deserves to receive you, the Lord God, with devotion, and in receiving you is filled with spiritual joy! Oh, how great a lord the soul receives! What a beloved guest she brings into her home! What a sweet companion she greets! What a faithful friend she welcomes! What a beautiful and noble spouse she embraces! I love you beyond all loves and beyond all desires!

My sweet beloved, let heaven and earth and all their array be silent in your presence, for whatever they have of loveliness and worth, they are all your gifts. They can never rise to the splendor of your name, whose wisdom is beyond all measure.

Chapter 4

**hat Many Good Things Are Given
to Those Who Devoutly Receive Communion**

Disciple:

My Lord God, give your sweet blessing to your servant so that I may be made worthy to approach your most generous Sacrament. Awaken my heart, and free me from this great apathy. Come to me with your saving grace that I may spiritually taste your sweetness, a sweetness which lies hidden at the very source of your Sacrament. Enlighten also my eyes, that I may gaze into so great a mystery, and strengthen me to believe it with a faith unclouded by doubt.

This is your work; we cannot do it. This is your sacred institution; it is not something we made up. No one can grasp and comprehend this mystery alone; it even soars beyond the subtle understanding of the angels. How can I, then, as unworthy as I am—a creature of mere dust and ashes—be able to probe into so profound a secret and understand it? O Lord, in the simplicity of my heart, in good and firm faith, and at your command I come to you with hope and reverence. I truly believe that you—God and man—are present here in the Sacrament. You want me to receive you; you want me to be one with you in love.

So I ask your mercy, and I beg you to give me a special grace that I may utterly dissolve in you and overflow with your love and never again seek anything apart from you. This most high and worthy Sacrament is the health of the soul and body, the medicine that cures every spiritual illness. In this Sacrament my weaknesses are cured and my passions are held in check, my temptations are overcome or they become less burdensome, grace is more greatly infused, virtue once started now increases, faith is made firm, hope is strengthened, and love's embers are fanned into flames, spreading ever wider.

O my God, protector of my soul, healer of human weakness, and giver of all inward comfort, you have given—and you continue to give—many good things in this Sacrament. Through it, you comfort your beloved people in every trial, and you lift them from the depths of dejection to the hope of your protection. You continually refresh and enlighten them with some new grace. Though they may at first have felt uneasy and unloving before Holy Communion, afterward they always find themselves changed for the better, having restored themselves with this heavenly food and drink.

You deal with your loved ones in this way so that they may truly admit and clearly experience their own weakness, so that they may acknowledge your great goodness and grace. Of themselves they are cold, hard, and without devotion; through your mercy they become fervent, eager and devout. Who can humbly approach the fountain of sweetness and not carry away a little taste of it? Who can stand near a blazing fire and not grow warm? You, Lord, are a fountain that is always full and overflowing, a fire that always burns and never dies out. If I may not draw from the fountain's fullness nor drink my fill, yet I shall place my mouth to the spout of that heavenly spring that I may sip from it a tiny drop to relieve my thirst and to keep me from drying up entirely.

And if I am not yet ready to be entirely heavenly and to burn as the cherubim and seraphim, I shall still try to apply myself to devotion and prepare my heart so that I may gain a small spark of divine fire by humbly receiving this life-giving Sacrament. Whatever is lacking in me, good Jesus, holy Savior, from your bounty and goodness, please supply it to me, for you have called each of us to you, saying: "Come to me all you who labor and are burdened, and I shall refresh you."

Indeed, I labor with great difficulty, and my heart is twisted with sorrow. I am crushed with sin, and I am unsettled by temptation. I am entangled and oppressed by my weaknesses, one on top of another. There is no one to help me, no one to set me free and save me, but you, Lord God, my Savior. I entrust myself and all that is mine to you, that you may protect me and lead me to eternal life.

You who have prepared your Body and Blood for my food and drink, receive me for the praise and glory of your name. Grant me, O Lord, God of my salvation, that by frequently receiving your mysteries the intensity of my love and devotion to you may ever increase.

Chapter 5

f the Dignity of the Sacrament and of the Priesthood

Jesus:

If you had the purity of angels and the holiness of St. John the Baptist, you would still not be worthy to receive this Sacrament, for it is not due to any human merits that a priest consecrates Christ's Sacrament and receives as food the bread of angels. Awesome is the ministry and great is the dignity of priests. Priests do what even angels cannot do! Only priests, duly ordained by the church, are able to celebrate Mass and consecrate the Body of Christ.

The priest is truly the minister of God, using the word of God at his command and institution, but God is present as the principal author and the invisible worker. All is subject to God as he wills; all obey as he commands. In this most excellent Sacrament, then, you ought to trust more in the all-powerful God than in your own opinion or in anything that you see. You should approach this Sacrament with profound awe and deep reverence. Take a look at yourself and see what ministry has been entrusted to you by the laying on of the bishop's hands. Look! you have been made a priest and have been consecrated to celebrate Mass. See that you offer the sacrifice to God faithfully and devoutly at the proper time, and see that your life is above reproach.

You have not lightened your burden by becoming a priest, you have increased it. A priest should shine in every virtue and should be a model for others. His path in life should not be an ordinary one, but one that leads to perfection and holiness. A priest wearing sacred vestments acts in Christ's place and humbly entreats God for himself and for all people. On his vestments he wears the sign of the Lord's cross before him and behind him that he may continually remember Christ's Passion. He carries the cross before him on the chasuble that he may carefully observe Christ's footsteps and fervently strive to follow them. He is sealed with the sign of the cross behind him that he may calmly suffer for God's sake whatever trials are laid upon him by others. He wears the cross in front that he may weep for his own sins, and he wears it in back that he may mourn for the sins of others, knowing all the while that he has been placed midway between God and the entire human family. A priest must never grow weary of prayer and the holy sacrifice until he has achieved grace and mercy.

When a priest celebrates Mass he honors God, delights the angels, builds the church, helps the living, assures rest for the dead, and shares in all good things.

Chapter 6

he Question of Preparing before Communion

Disciple:

O Lord, when I ponder your greatness and my unworthiness, I am badly shaken and confused, for if I do not receive you in Holy Communion, I shun life, and if I receive you unworthily, I offend you. So, what shall I do, my God, my helper, my advisor in every need? Teach me the right way. Show me what to do to prepare for Holy Communion. It is important that I know how to ready my heart, that I may devoutly and reverently receive your Sacrament for my well-being. It is important if I am to celebrate so great and sacred a sacrifice.

Chapter 7

f Examining One's Conscience, and of Planning to Change for the Better

Jesus:

Above all else a priest of God should come to celebrate, to handle and to receive this Sacrament with deep humility and profound reverence, with full faith and with the firm intention of honoring God. Examine your conscience carefully, and cleanse and purify it as best you can by being truly sorry for your sins and by humbly confessing them. If you do so, nothing will weigh on your conscience, and nothing will cause remorse that may keep you from me. Be sorry for all of your sins in general; in particular, regret your daily offenses, and be especially sorry for them. If you have time, confess to God in the secret recesses of your heart the pain that your failings have caused you. Bemoan and be full of sorrow that you are such a divided person, so alive to your passions, so full of lust, so volatile in your feelings, so entangled with foolish notions, so inclined to gratifying yourself, so neglectful of your inner life, so prone to the collapse of your moral resolve, so ready to avoid your own conscience, so ready to relax, so slow to rigor and zeal, so curious to listen to gossip and waste time, so remiss in embracing the humble and poor, so greedy in getting, so stingy in giving, so tight-fisted in keeping, so inconsiderate in what you say, so reluctant in keeping silent, so undisciplined in behavior, so rash in what you do, so ready in eating, so deaf to God's word, so quick to rest, so slow to work, so awake to hear stories, so sleepy at vigils, so eager for devotions to end, so wandering in attention, so negligent in reciting the Office, so indifferent in celebrating Mass, so matter-of-fact in receiving Holy Communion, so quickly distracted, so seldom at one with yourself, so suddenly moved to anger, so easily offended by others, so prone to judge, so harsh in correcting others, so happy in good times, so depressed in bad times, so often making good resolutions, and so reluctant in carrying them out.

After you have confessed these failings—and your others, too—and after you have felt sorry for them and have expressed great remorse, firmly resolve to change your life and to do better. Then, by the complete resignation of your will, offer yourself to me as a perpetual sacrifice on the altar of your heart. Faithfully entrust your body and soul to me, so that you may become worthy to approach my altar to offer sacrifice to God and to receive the Sacrament of my Body for your salvation.

There is no offering more worthy—no satisfaction greater—for the washing away of sins than to offer yourself purely and completely to God at the same time that the Body of Christ is offered in the Mass and in Communion. If a person does all that he can do and resolves from the very bottom of his heart to change his ways, then as often as he comes to me for pardon and grace I shall give it to him, saying: "As I live, I do not want the death of the sinner. I want him to turn from his ways and live. I shall no longer remember his sins; all will be forgiven him."

Chapter 8

**f Christ's Offering on the Cross,
and of Our Own Self-Surrender**

Jesus:

With my hands outstretched on the cross and my body naked, I freely offered myself to God the Father for your sins. Nothing was left in me that was not given to God. In the very same way—with all your strength and love—you too should willingly offer yourself to me each day in the Mass as a pure and holy offering.

What more do I ask of you than yourself? I do not care at all for anything else that you may give me. I do not seek your gift. I seek you.

Just as it would not satisfy you to have anything but me, so it does not please me to have anything you may give, if you do not give yourself. Offer yourself to me and give your entire self for God. Such an offering will be accepted. Look, I offered all of myself to the Father for you. I gave my entire Body and Blood for your food so that I might be all yours and you might be all mine. If you hold back and will not resign yourself to my will without having second thoughts, then your offering is not perfect nor will we become perfectly at one.

So, if you wish to achieve a free spirit and gain my grace, everything you do must be preceded by a spontaneous offering of yourself into the hands of God. This is why so few people become enlightened and inwardly free: Most do not know how to give themselves to me completely. I have said this, and I mean it: "Unless a person renounces all that he has, he cannot be my follower." So, if you wish to be my disciple, give yourself to me with your whole heart.

Chapter 9

**hat We Ought to Offer Ourselves
and All That Is Ours to God,
and That We Ought to Pray for All Others**

Disciple:

O Lord, all things in heaven and on earth are yours. I wish to give myself to you as a voluntary offering and to remain forever yours. Lord, in the simplicity of my heart I offer myself to you today as your servant until the end of time. I wish to serve you in humble obedience and as a gift of eternal praise. Receive me, together with this holy sacrifice of your precious Body which I offer to you today in the presence of your angels—your unseen helpers, that it may benefit me and contribute toward the salvation of all your people.

Lord, on your altar of forgiveness I offer you all of the sins and offenses which I have committed in your sight and in the sight of your holy angels from the day that I was first capable of sin right up to this present hour. Burn them and consume them all in the fire of your love. Remove the stains of my sin and cleanse my conscience. Restore your grace to me, which I lost by sin, forgiving everything and mercifully adopting me into your family with a kiss of peace.

What can I do with my sins except humbly confess them and weep for them and forever beg your forgiveness? O my God, mercifully hear me as I stand before you and earnestly ask this of you. All of my sins are repugnant to me. I do not want to commit them ever again. I am sorry for them, and I shall regret them as long as I live. I am ready to do penance for them and to make satisfaction as best I can.

Forgive me, O God, forgive me my sins through your holy name. Save my soul, which you have ransomed with your precious Blood. Look at me, Lord! I place myself at your mercy; I yield myself into your hands. Deal with me according to your goodness and not as my evil and crooked ways deserve.

I offer to you also all the good that I have done, however poor and flawed it may be. Transform it and make it holy that it may be pleasing in your sight and worthy of being offered to you. Continually draw me on to better things. Guide me, lazy and unworthy person that I am, to a blessed and praiseworthy end.

I offer you, too, all the holy desires of many devout people: the needs of my parents, friends, brothers, sisters and all of those who are dear to me. I offer you the needs of those who, for love of you, have helped either me or others, and I offer you the prayers and Masses that others have asked me to say for themselves and their loved ones, both living and dead. May they all feel your grace, your comfort, your protection from danger, and the freedom that you may grant them from pain. May they offer you joyful and generous thanks for hearing their prayers.

I also offer you my prayers and the sacrifice of this Mass, especially for those who have in some way offended, grieved, or insulted me or who have caused me any loss or hurt. Likewise, I offer my prayers for all those whom I have at one time or another grieved, troubled, injured, or shamed by what I said or did, knowingly or unknowingly. Forgive us our offenses, and forgive those who offend us.

O Lord, remove from our hearts all suspicion, indignation, anger and contention, and whatever else may harm charity and lessen broth-

erly love. Have mercy, Lord, on those who ask your mercy. Grant your
grace to those without it, and help us to live that we might be worthy of
it. Help us, Lord, to continue on to eternal life. Amen.

Chapter 10

hat Holy Communion Is Not to Be Lightly Omitted

Jesus:

You should have frequent recourse to the fountain of grace and divine mercy, to the fountain of goodness and perfect purity. Like a balm
for your soul, Holy Communion will help you to overcome your weaknesses and bad habits, so that you may be stronger and more watchful
against all the temptations and deceits of the devil. The enemy, knowing
the goodness and great healing power of Holy Communion, constantly
tries, with every means at his disposal, to get in the way and prevent the
faithful and devout from receiving it. In fact, some people, while preparing themselves for Holy Communion, are subject to Satan's worst
attacks. This wicked spirit, as it is written in Job, comes among the children of God to trouble them with his usual nasty behavior, bullying
them and confusing them so as to lessen their devotion. By repeated attacks, he tries to undermine their faith so that they may either give up
going to Communion altogether or receive it with little enthusiasm and
devotion. Ignore his tricks and the pictures he paints in your mind, no
matter how disgusting and horrid they may be. Hurl all the foul images
back on his head! The wretch is to be scorned and despised! You should
not fail to go to Holy Communion because of his taunts or because of
any fuss he causes.

Often some people are held back from going to Holy Communion
because they feel that they are not devout enough or because of an excessive anxiety about going to confession. If this is your concern, follow
the counsel of a wise person and put anxiety and scruple aside. Such
concerns get in the way of God's grace and destroy any devout thoughts
you may have.

Do not put off Holy Communion for any trivial qualm or small concern, but go quickly to confess it, and freely forgive all those who have offended you. If you have offended anyone, humbly ask forgiveness, and God will freely pardon you. What good does it do you to put off confession or to assign Communion to another day? Cleanse yourself right away. Spit out the poison quickly. Make haste to take the medicine and you will feel better than if you were to wait for a long time. If today you put aside Holy Communion for one reason, tomorrow may bring another more serious one, and so you may be kept from Communion for a long while, feeling less and less fit for it as the days go by. Get rid of this sloth and laziness as quickly as you can, for it does no good at all to linger in uneasiness and anxiety and to deprive yourself of the divine mysteries because of everyday obstacles. In fact, you do yourself even more harm by putting off Holy Communion for a long time, for it usually leads to serious apathy.

Sadly, some people who are indifferent and not firmly committed eagerly look for excuses for putting off confession. They simply want to postpone Holy Communion so that they will not have to keep a greater watch over themselves. Oh, what little love and feeble devotion they have who so easily put off Holy Communion! A person who lives his life as God wishes and who keeps his conscience pure is pleasing to God and makes him happy. Such a person could receive Communion at every opportunity—and would want to—if he could do so without attracting too much attention. If a person sometimes abstains from Communion out of humility or because of some legitimate obstacle, he should be praised for his reverence. But if laziness steals over him, he must arouse himself and do all he can to shake it off. If he does, the Lord will help him, for he looks with special favor on our good intentions. When he is honestly prevented from Communion, however, let him always have a good will and the holy intention of sharing in the Body and Blood of Christ. In this way he will not miss the benefit of the Sacrament, for every day and every hour any devout person can freely share in an intimate fellowship with Christ. Nevertheless, on certain days and at appointed times he ought to receive sacramentally the Body of his Redeemer with loving reverence and seek the praise and honor of God more than his own spiritual comfort. As often as a person meditates on the mystery of Christ's Incarnation and Passion, so often does he communicate with him in a mystical way and so often is he refreshed by Christ and enflamed with love for him. On the other hand, a person who does not prepare himself unless a feast is at hand or because preparation is not his habit will often find himself unprepared.

Blessed is that person who offers himself as a sacrifice to the Lord whenever he celebrates Mass or receives Holy Communion. When celebrating Mass neither drag it out nor say it too fast. Celebrate it according to the common practice of those with whom you live. In celebrating Mass, you should not be a source of irritation or tedium to others, but you should stick to the ordinary ways common to your community. Seek to be helpful to others, rather than to indulge your own preferences.

Chapter 11

hat the Body of Christ and the Holy Scriptures Are Most Necessary to the Faithful Soul

Disciple:

O sweet Lord Jesus, how great is the delight of a devout soul that feasts with you at your banquet where no other food is set before her but yourself, her only beloved. You are more to be wished for than all that her heart can desire. For me, it would be sweet to sit in your presence and weep tears of love from the very depth of my being and with the holy Magdalene wash your feet with them.

But where is this devotion? Where is this flood of holy tears? Surely, in your sight and in the sight of your holy angels, my whole heart should burn and weep for joy. You are truly present to me in the Sacrament, though hidden beneath a different form, for my eyes could not endure to see you in your own divine brightness nor could the whole world resist your splendor. In concealing yourself beneath the Sacrament you consider my weakness. I truly possess and adore him whom the angels in heaven adore, but I see him only through the eyes of faith; they see him as he is, unveiled. I must be satisfied with the light of true faith and walk in it until the day when eternal light breaks through and shadowy figures pass away.

But when that which is perfect comes, the need for sacraments will end, for the blessed, who are in heavenly glory, do not need the medicine of the sacraments. They rejoice endlessly in God's presence, seeing his glory face to face, and being transformed from one degree of brightness into the brightness of the unfathomable deity, they taste the word of God made flesh, as he was in the beginning, as he is now, and as he ever shall be.

The thought of these wonders makes even spiritual comforts seem wearisome to me, for as long as I cannot clearly see my Lord in his glory, all else that I see or hear means nothing to me. You are my witness, O God, that nothing can comfort me, that nothing can bring me rest, but you, my God, whom I wish to contemplate for all of eternity.

But this is not possible yet. I must strive, then, to achieve great patience and to keep you always foremost in my mind. Your saints, Lord, who now rejoice with you in the kingdom of heaven, waited in faith and great patience for you. What they believed, I believe. What they hoped for, I hope for. Where they have arrived, I, by your grace, also hope to arrive. In the meantime, I shall walk in faith, comforted by the examples of the saints. I shall have holy books, too, for comfort and to mirror life. Beyond all these, I shall have your most holy Body for my sole remedy and refuge.

I firmly believe that two things are utterly essential for me in this life; without them this journey would be unbearable to me: They are food and light. So, in my weakness you have given me your holy Body for refreshing my mind and body, and you have given me your word as a lantern for my feet. Without these two things I could not do a very good job of living; God's word is the light of my soul, and your Sacrament is the bread of life.

These may also be called two tables placed on either side of the treasury of holy church. One table is the holy altar, having the holy bread, that is, the precious Body of Christ. The other table is the divine law, containing holy teachings that show us the correct interpretation of faith and lead us onward through the inner veil into the Holy of Holies.

Thanks be to you, Lord Jesus, light of eternal light, for the table of sacred teaching, which you have given to us through your servants, the prophets, apostles and other teachers. Thanks be to you, Creator and Redeemer of us all, who, to declare your love to the whole world, have prepared a great supper in which you have set before us not a figurative lamb, but your most sacred Body and Blood. By preparing this sacred banquet, you bring joy to all the faithful, filling them with the cup of salvation, which contains all the delights of paradise. The holy angels feast with us too, and their happiness is even greater than ours.

Oh, how great and honorable is the office of priests! They have been given the ability to consecrate, with sacred words, the Lord of majesty, to bless him with their lips, to hold him with their hands, to receive him with their own mouths, and to give him to others. Oh, how clean those hands should be, how pure the mouth, how holy the body, how spotless the heart of a priest, to whom so often enters the author of purity. From the mouth of a priest, who so often receives the Sacrament of Christ, should come not a word that is not holy, upright, and helpful. Since he is accustomed to look upon the Body of Christ, his eyes should be simple and modest. The hands that touch the creator of heaven and earth should be pure and lifted up to heaven. What is said in the Law is meant especially for priests: "Be holy, for I, the Lord your God, am holy."

Almighty God, by your grace help us, we who have undertaken the priestly office, that we may be able to serve you worthily, devoutly and with all purity and good conscience. If we are unable to live in such innocence as we should, grant us the grace to weep for the wrongs we have done and, in a spirit of humility and resolve, grant that we may serve you with greater zeal as we journey through life.

Chapter 12

hat Receiving Christ in Holy Communion Requires Preparation

Jesus:

I am the lover of purity and the giver of all holiness. I seek a pure heart, and there I shall rest. Prepare a large, furnished upper room for me, and I shall celebrate my resurrection with you and my disciples. If you want me to come and stay with you, clear away the old yeast and clean up that place in your heart where you live. For a time, shut out the world and all its confusion and noise; sit like a sparrow alone on a housetop, and in the sorrow of your soul, think of the many times that you have turned your back on God and have gone your own way.

Every lover prepares the best and most beautiful room in the house for his beloved, for in this way he shows his affection for the one he loves. Understand, though, that you cannot properly prepare yourself by your own efforts no matter how worthy they may be, even if you were to spend an entire year trying, and even if you were to think of nothing else! It is only out of my goodness and grace that you are allowed to approach my table. It is as if a beggar were invited to dinner by a very rich person and he had nothing to give in return for the kindness except humility and thanks.

Do what you can and do it attentively, not out of habit or because you feel that you must. Instead, prepare yourself with deep awe, profound reverence and unutterable love to receive the Body of your Lord God who sees fit to come to you. It is I who have called you, I who have wished it to be done. I shall provide what is lacking in you. Come and receive me.

When I give you the grace of devotion give thanks to your God. I give it to you not because you deserve it, but because I have been merciful toward you. If you do not have this grace but instead feel yourself to be dry, keep on praying, sighing and knocking at my door. Do not give up until you are made worthy of receiving some crumb or drop of saving grace. You need me; I do not need you. You do not make me holy, but I come to make you holy and to make you a better person. You come to be made holy by me and to be made one with me, to receive new grace, and to renew your resolve to change your life. Do not neglect this grace, but prepare your heart with all diligence, and welcome your beloved to share it with you.

You must not only devoutly prepare yourself before Communion, but you should also take great care to stay in a devout state after receiving the Sacrament. Vigilance is no less required after Communion than devout preparation is required before. Keeping a close watch on yourself after receiving Communion is the best preparation for gaining even greater grace in the future. If you immediately turn your mind from God to your own affairs after Communion, you will find yourself all the more unprepared to receive God's grace. Stay quiet. Live calmly in the secret recesses of your heart and enjoy your God, for you have him, and the whole world cannot take him away from you. I am the one to whom you should give your entire being, so that freed from all care, you no longer live for yourself, but for me.

Chapter 13

hat a Devout Soul Should Wish Wholeheartedly to Be United with Christ in the Sacrament

Disciple:

Who will allow me to be alone with you, Lord, to open my whole heart to you, and to enjoy you as my soul desires? Let no one think little of me nor anyone disturb or concern me. You alone speak to me and I to you, as a lover speaks to a loved one and as a friend shares a meal with a friend. This I pray for and this I desire: that I may be totally united to you, and that you may fill my entire heart. May I increasingly acquire a taste for heavenly and eternal things by receiving Holy Communion and by frequently celebrating Mass.

O Lord God, when will I be wholly united to you, completely absorbed in you, and totally forgetful of myself? You in me, and I in you! Grant that we may remain together forever! Truly, you are my beloved, chosen from among thousands. My soul is pleased to dwell with you all the days of her life. Truly, you are the source of my peace. Supreme peace and true rest lie in you, and outside of you there is only toil, sorrow and endless misery. Truly, you are the hidden God. You have nothing to do with the wicked, but you speak to those who are humble and simple. Oh, how sweet is your spirit, Lord. To show your sweetness toward your children, you saw fit to refresh them with the most sweet bread that comes down from heaven. Truly, there is no other nation so great, no other nation so intimate with its gods, as you, our God, are intimate with us. For our daily comfort you raise our hearts to heaven, and you give yourself to be eaten and enjoyed.

What people are so highly favored as those whom you love? Or what creature under heaven is so beloved as the devout soul to whom you come and feed with your glorious Body? O inexpressible grace! O admirable graciousness! O boundless love, bestowed on the entire human family!

What can I give back to the Lord for this grace and for his great love? There is nothing I can give that is more acceptable than to offer my whole heart to my God and to join myself intimately to him. When my soul is perfectly at one with God, then I shall rejoice from the very depths of my being. Then he will say to me: "If you want to be with me, then I want to be with you." And I shall answer him: "See fit, Lord, to remain with me. I shall gladly stay with you." That my heart be united with you is my one and only desire.

Chapter 14

 f the Ardent Desire of Some Devout People to Receive the Body of Christ

Disciple:

Oh, how great and abundant is your sweetness, Lord, which you have reserved for those who love you as they should! When I call to mind some devout people who approach your Sacrament with such great devotion and love, Lord, I burn with shame that I approach your altar and the table of Holy Communion so cold and indifferent. Why do I remain so dry and have so little love in my heart? Why am I not burning with love in your presence, my God? Why am I not as strongly drawn to you and as profoundly affected as many of those who love you are? Because of their overwhelming desire for Communion and the tenderness of their hearts they cannot hold back their tears! With their entire beings they long for you from their very depths, O God, fountain of life. They are unable to satisfy their hunger in any other way except by receiving your Body with all delight and spiritual longing.

O true, burning faith of theirs! It serves as an argument to prove your sacred presence! They truly know their Lord in the breaking of the bread. Their hearts burn so strongly in them because Jesus walks with them. Such affection and devotion, such overpowering love and passion, are often beyond me.

O good, sweet and merciful Jesus, be merciful to me, and let me feel, at least sometimes, a little of that same heartfelt love for you when I receive Holy Communion. If you do, my faith will be strengthened more, my hope in your goodness will be increased, and my love, set on fire by having tasted the heavenly food, will never fail. Your mercy is so powerful that it can give me the grace I desire. Whenever you like you can grant me this gift. Although I do not burn with such great passion as those who are especially devout, yet, by your grace, I wish to have that same intense and burning desire as they have. I hope and pray that I may be counted among your devout lovers and be numbered in their holy company.

Chapter 15

hat the Grace of Devotion Is Gained by Humility

Jesus:

You should seek persistently the grace of devotion, ask for it earnestly, look for it patiently and confidently, accept it thankfully, hold on to it humbly, use it with care, and leave the time and manner of this heavenly visit to God until he comes to join you. Above all, when you feel little or no inner devotion, you should feel great humility, but not to the point where you become overly dejected or too sad. God often gives in a flash what he has held back for a long time. He sometimes gives at the end of prayer what he delayed giving at the beginning.

If grace were always given at once and were yours for the asking, human weakness could not deal with it. So you must wait for the grace of devotion with firm hope and with humble patience. When it is not given to you or when it is mysteriously taken away, blame yourself and your sins. Sometimes it is a little thing that hinders grace or keeps it hidden from you—if, indeed, that may be called little and not great which keeps such a great good from you. But if you remove the obstacle—small or large—and fully overcome it, you will get what you ask. As soon as you yield yourself to God with your whole heart, not seeking this or that for your own pleasure or will but placing yourself entirely in his hands, you will find yourself quickly at one with God and at peace. Nothing will give you greater happiness or please you so much as being obedient to the divine will.

Therefore, if you lift up your mind to God with a singleness of heart and if you empty yourself of all that is not God, you will become fit to receive his grace and to live a life of love and devotion. The Lord gives this blessing where he finds the vessel empty. So, the more completely you pour out your self-centeredness and the demands that it makes upon you, and the more completely you become empty and wholly dependent on God's love, the more quickly will grace come to you. When at last you can place yourself in God's hands without any reservations, your heart will overflow with joy and wonder, knowing that the Lord is with you, both now and forever.

So, there you have it! The person who seeks God with his whole heart shall be blessed; he does not have a soul for nothing. In receiving the Holy Eucharist, such a person wins the great grace of divine union because he does not focus on his own devotion and comfort, but goes beyond all devotion and comfort and seeks the glory and honor of God.

Chapter 16

hat We Should Make Our Needs Known to Christ and Ask for His Help

Disciple:

O most sweet and loving Lord, whom I now devoutly wish to receive, you know my weaknesses and my needs. You know how many bad habits and vices I have. You know how often I am burdened, tempted, shaken and stained by sin. I come to you for healing. I pray to you for comfort and support. I speak to you, who know all things, to whom all my inmost thoughts are evident. You alone can adequately comfort me and help me. You know what good things I need most, and you know how poor I am in virtue.

Look! I stand before you poor and naked, asking your grace and imploring your mercy. Feed me, for I am hungry. Inflame my coldness with the fire of your love. Illuminate my blindness with the light of your presence. Turn my eyes from all that is not you; turn all oppression into patience. Make all that leads me from you not worth thinking about. Make me forget it all. Lift up my heart to you in heaven, and let me not wander aimlessly about the world. From now on, you will be my only delight, for you alone are my food and drink, my love and joy, my sweetness and my whole good.

Oh, that by your presence you would set me fully on fire, totally consume me and transform me into you, so that through the grace of inner union and by melting in love's flames I would become one spirit with you. Do not leave me hungry and thirsty, but treat me mercifully as you have so often and so admirably treated your saints. How wonderful it would be if I were burned and wholly consumed for you, since you are a fire always burning and never consumed, a love that purifies the heart and enlightens the mind.

Chapter 17

 f Burning Love and the Strong Desire to Receive Christ

Disciple:

O Lord, I long to receive you with deep devotion and burning love, with all the affection and fervor of my heart. Just as many saints and devout persons, who were especially pleasing to you because of their holy lives and ardent devotion, longed to receive you in Holy Communion, so do I long to receive you, too. O my God, eternal Love, my entire good and endless happiness, I wish to receive you with the same burning desire and profound reverence that any of the saints ever had or ever could have felt.

Although I am not worthy to have these devout feelings, nevertheless, I give all the affection of my heart to you, as if I were the only one who had all these pleasing and burning desires. In fact, whatever a pious mind can think of and desire, all this I present and offer to you with the greatest reverence and deepest love. I do not want to hold anything back for myself. I want to sacrifice myself and all that is mine freely and deliberately to you.

O Lord, my God, my Creator and my Redeemer, I wish to receive you today with the same tenderness, reverence, praise and honor; with the same thankfulness, dignity, and affection; with the same faith, hope, and unblemished love as your most holy mother, the glorious Virgin Mary. Let me receive you as she did, when the angel announced to her the mystery of your Incarnation and she humbly and devoutly replied: "Behold, the handmaid of the Lord. Let it be done to me according to your word."

As your blessed precursor, John the Baptist, rejoiced in your presence and leaped with the joy of the Holy Spirit while he was still in his mother's womb, let me also be enflamed with an intense and holy desire for you. And as when he saw Jesus walking among us, let me say with equal love and humility: "The bridegroom's friend, who stands and hears him, rejoices with gladness at his voice." Like John the Baptist, the most excellent among your saints, let me offer myself to you with all my heart.

I bring to you the joy of all devout hearts, their burning love, soaring thoughts, divine insights and heavenly visions. I place before you all the virtues and praises that have been or ever will be given to you by all the creatures of heaven and earth. I do this for myself and for all those who have been commended to me in prayer, so that by every one of them you may be praised and glorified forever and ever.

Accept my vows, O Lord, my God, and my desires of giving you unending praise and endless blessing, which are due to you because of your exceeding greatness. This I give to you and wish to give to you every day and every moment. I invite and ask all the heavenly spirits and all the faithful to join me in offering you thanks and praise.

Let all peoples, nations and languages, with great joy and deep devotion, praise you and magnify your holy and sweet name. Let all those who with reverence and devotion celebrate your most high Sacrament and receive it with full faith, deserve to find grace and mercy before you, and may they humbly pray for me, a sinner. And after they have won the grace of devotion and the reward of being at one with you, and after they have left the heavenly table full of comfort and wondrously refreshed, may they see fit to remember poor me.

Chapter 18

hat We Should Not Pry into This Sacrament Out of Curiosity

Jesus:

You should guard against curious and useless prying into this most profound Sacrament if you do not want to sink into an abyss of doubt. The person who probes into majesty will be overwhelmed by its glory. God can do more than you can understand. A pious and humble inquiry into truth is all right as long as you are always willing to be taught and to walk in the sound teachings of the Fathers. Blessed is that simplicity that leaves the difficult paths of questioning and walks along the plain and firm road of God's commandments. Many people have lost all feeling of devotion because they wanted to pry into profound things. It is faith and a genuine, honest life that is required of you, not a lofty intellect nor a deep understanding of God's mysteries. If you do not understand or fully grasp those things that are below you, how will you comprehend those that are above you? So, submit yourself to God and rely on your faith, and you will receive all the knowledge that you need.

Some people are horribly tempted about the faith and this Sacrament. It is not their fault, but the devil's. Pay no attention to such temptations, and do not argue with your thoughts or try to answer the doubts that the devil whispers in your ear. Instead, believe in God's words and believe his saints and prophets, and the wicked enemy will turn tail and run. It will often do you much good to suffer such doubts. The devil does not tempt unbelievers and sinners; he surely possesses them already. It is the faithful and devout whom he tempts and molests, and he does it in a variety of ways.

So, continue on in your simple and staunch faith and come to the Sacrament with humble reverence and securely commit to almighty God all that you cannot understand. God does not mislead you, but a person is lost who places too much trust in himself. God walks with simple people and reveals himself to those who are humble. He gives understanding to the little ones and opens the minds of the pure; he hides his grace from the curious and the arrogant.

Human reason is weak and can be misled; true faith, on the other hand, cannot be fooled. All reasoning and natural inquiry should follow faith, not precede it or weaken it. In this most holy and most excellent Sacrament, faith and love excel, and they work in hidden ways. God— eternal, boundless, and of infinite power—does great things in heaven and on earth that are a complete mystery to us. There is no searching out his wondrous works. If God's works were such that human reason could easily figure them out, they could not be said to be wonderful, nor would they be far too marvelous for words to express.